NEW
LOVE

THINKING ALOUD ABOUT PRACTICAL HOLINESS

D1445538

Also by Shaw Clifton:

What Does The Salvationist Say? (London, The Salvation Army, 1977).

Growing Together (London, The Salvation Army, 1984). With Helen Clifton.

Strong Doctrine, Strong Mercy (London, The Salvation Army, 1985).

Never The Same Again (Alexandria VA, Crest Books, 1997).

Who Are These Salvationists? (Alexandria VA, Crest Books, 1999).

Available from Flag Publications:

Touched with Splendour by Cyril R. Bradwell (Wellington, Flag Publications, 2003).

NEW LOVE

THINKING ALOUD ABOUT PRACTICAL HOLINESS

by Shaw Clifton
and international guest writers

FLAG
PUBLICATIONS

The Salvation Army
New Zealand Fiji and Tonga Territory

New Love

Published by Flag Publications

The Salvation Army

New Zealand Fiji and Tonga Territory

PO Box 6015

Wellington, New Zealand

© 2004 The Territorial Commander
The Salvation Army, New Zealand

ISBN 0-476-00345-8

Cover Design: Emily Fletcher

Layout: Andrew Killick

Produced by Castle Publishing Services

info@castlepublishing.biz

www.castlepublishing.biz

Printed in New Zealand by Wentforth Print

Second printing 2006

All scripture quotations, unless otherwise indicated,
are taken from the HOLY BIBLE,
NEW INTERNATIONAL VERSION®. NIV®.
Copyright © 1973, 1978, 1984
by International Bible Society.
Used by permission of Zondervan.
All rights reserved.

For my father

CONTENTS

Part II
by International Guest Contributors

INTRODUCTION

THE modern Salvation Army is still a 'sanctification Army', even if some in our ranks have forgotten it, and even if those beyond our ranks do not always notice it. The real possibility of living a sanctified life, victorious over sin and temptation, is encapsulated in our Tenth Doctrine and can be heard expounded in many (though not all) parts of the Army world on a regular basis.

This volume of essays does not set out to expound the doctrine but instead assumes its truth and practicability. For those seeking a systematic exposition of our teaching on sanctification and on the blessing of a clean heart I recommend the Army's 'Handbook of Doctrine' in the successive editions published in 1940, 1969 and 1998. Each edition is helpful, but the earliest offers the most compelling and life-challenging read.

New Love is not a 'how to' book. It has come about because, in the words of the incomparable Commissioner Samuel Logan Brengle, the various writers 'desire with unutterable longings to bless and help'. It was Franz Kafka who said, 'A book must be the axe for the frozen sea inside us.' So our aim is to encourage readers to plumb afresh the universal relevance and applicability of Wesleyan holiness, and to demonstrate, by a wide choice of everyday themes and topics, the down-to- earth nature of holiness teaching, of which we in the Army are blessed still to be inheritors and stewards.

The Army's Crest Books label in the United States of America deserves much credit for the 2003 publication of Robert Rightmire's splendid

Sanctified Sanity. That scholarly, yet eminently readable, account of Brengle's life and holiness teaching has already brought to many of us a renewed, timely emphasis on our holiness heritage. The present volume hopes to build upon that publication and offers an unpretentious, pastorally motivated collection of essays for Salvationists and others to consider.

The aim has been to produce a book that is stimulating, readable, and accessible in both style and content. For that reason, and to allow the text to flow, detailed footnotes and references have not been included.

Some of the essays may appear to contain mildly controversial material. It is the writers who take responsibility for any views expressed. Nothing purports to be an official statement for The Salvation Army, unless so labelled.

I am deeply indebted to my distinguished guest contributors for their ready response to my invitation to write for this volume. All are officers of The Salvation Army. They represent a wide range of experience, ranks, ages and nationalities, but in each of them there beats a heart in which William Booth and Samuel Brengle would have taken delight. Their literary styles vary widely, adding interest to the book. Challenge, flair and thrust abound. I feel especially blessed to be able to include contributions from three younger officers (Court, Ryan and Clifton) who write with articulate passion about holiness. Clearly, all is not lost.

Lt. Colonel Marlene Chase, Literary Secretary and Editor-in-Chief at the USA National Headquarters, has been a strong source of encouragement since the earliest days of this project. My private secretary in Wellington, Major Joyce Langdon, with her gift of helpfulness, has given extra mile clerical support. I record warm thanks also to the Literature Council of the New Zealand, Fiji and Tonga Territory in Wellington.

Without the constancy and understanding of Helen, my wife, this volume would never have seen the light of day. Our son, Captain Matt Clifton, as well as providing a chapter of his own, has provided penetrating comment along the way and has saved me from many an error. Jenny and Marcus Collings, our daughter and son-in-law, have also made most helpful input. I take sole responsibility for opinions expressed in my chapters and for any errors that remain throughout the volume.

The day by day prayers and weekly airmail letters of my aged father, Major Albert Clifton (R), have made an incalculable contribution to my life and it is to him, with love, admiration and gratitude for his unassuming example of holy living, that I dedicate the pages within these covers.

Shaw Clifton
Wellington, New Zealand
March 2004

QUOTATIONS TO PONDER

I am the Lord your God; consecrate yourselves and be holy,
because I am holy.
Leviticus 11:44

If we confess our sins, He is faithful and just
and will forgive us our sins and purify us from all unrighteousness.
1 John 1:9

'Neath the searching light of Heaven,
Here a deeper truth I see;
Though the past was long forgiven,
One more chain must yet be riven,
Lord, from self I am not free.
Ruth Tracy

Though you know your sins forgiven,
Greater things await you still;
Freedom here from sin's dominion,
Power to do the Master's will.
Fear no danger, he is with you,
Let no foe your steps arrest;

Seek today the Father's blessing,
Enter now the land of rest.
Walter Windybank

Holiness of life is the only true evidence of a saving faith.
Hannah More

Sanctification is to be intensely focussed on God's point of view.
Oswald Chambers

A pure heart will improve your judgement.
The Holy Spirit will be your teacher.
Samuel Logan Brengle

There is no ceiling on goodness.
Anon.

A pure heart will give you peace. You must not expect
a life of uninterrupted gladness in this world … but peace is
your birthright, and with a pure heart,
the treasure shall be yours.
William Booth

Be filled with the Spirit.
Ephesians 5:18

*What do I mean by a holy life? It is ... a life fashioned after
the life of the Lord Jesus Christ. Is not such a life desirable?*
William Booth

*Since we have these promises, dear friends,
let us purify ourselves from everything that
contaminates body and spirit,
perfecting holiness out of reverence for God.*
2 Corinthians 7:1

*Holiness for you and for me is not maturity, but purity:
a clean heart in which the Holy Spirit dwells,
filling it with pure, tender and constant love to God and man.*
Samuel Logan Brengle

*The law of the Christian is Christ Himself in Person.
In Him we have life and therefore also the law of our life.*
Bernard Haring

*To attend to holiness is to attend to a matter that lies
at the very heart of what it means to be and become fully human.*
Stephen C. Barton

*Holiness is God's way of providing a remedy for sin –
an antidote in this life for its poison, a healing for its disease,
a restoration for its destruction.*
Florence Booth

Nothing on earth do I desire
But thy pure love within my breast...
Antoinette Bourignon, trs John Wesley

We believe that it is the privilege of all believers
to be wholly sanctified, and that their whole spirit and soul and body
may be preserved blameless unto the coming of our Lord Jesus Christ.
Doctrine 10 of The Salvation Army

Jesus has died to purchase this uttermost salvation,
and it is your Heavenly Father's will for you, just now.
Have faith in God, give yourself utterly to him, even now,
and begin to seek the blessing with a determination
never to stop seeking until it is yours,
and you shall not be long without it.
Samuel Logan Brengle

PART
ONE

SALVATIONISM

HOLINESS AND THE NON-NEGOTIABLES OF SALVATIONISM

A crucial and basic distinction

THE challenge rang out: 'Has not The Salvation Army passed its sell-by date?' I was being called to account in a public setting. It felt as though the Army was on trial and I was to be her defending advocate. The Lord helped me. It was necessary first to clarify the question. It turned out that those asking it knew quite a bit about the Army. They knew our structures and methods, our doctrines and policies. So it was not so much a question about The Salvation Army as an organisation, but more an attempt to tease out the nature of Salvationism. It is important not to confuse The Salvation Army with Salvationism.

If 'The Salvation Army' is the ecclesial body known by that name, the vast international organisation that is both evangelical church and social service agency (see the writer's *Who Are These Salvationists? – An Analysis for the 21st Century* (Alexandria, Crest Books, 1999)), then 'Salvationism' is the sum total or combination of various distinctive characteristics that are peculiar to the Army. Salvationism is a word that denotes certain attitudes, a particular worldview. It signifies an amalgam of beliefs, stances, commitments, callings that when taken together cannot be found in any other body, religious or secular.

The challenge thus became: 'Has *Salvationism* passed its sell-by date?' To answer adequately meant teasing out the elusive meaning of Salvationism. 'What is Salvationism?' is not the same question as 'What is The Salvation Army?' The latter can be answered pretty well by reference to our history, our methods, and our structures. Salvationism on the other hand is the thing that underlies and undergirds all of that. It is what makes us who we are. It is about our pulse, our heartbeat. It is about the non-negotiables that make us a distinctive people, called out by God. (In this essay I am using 'non-negotiables' and 'distinctives' as synonyms.)

Salvationism was invented by God. The Salvation Army was raised up by God who then entrusted Salvationism to it as a sacred trust. The Army is thus the divinely appointed steward of Salvationism. As already said, it is important not to confuse the one with the other.

This essay is therefore an attempt to restate the essentials of Salvationism. Holiness will be right at the centre of that restatement.

Obedience to God

It is still important to be able to articulate our distinctives as a Christian body. Voices which today call for less attention to be placed upon special denominational characteristics ought not to be allowed to deflect us. It is true that denominationalism can be, and often has been, a harmful barrier between Christians. In North America, for example, there are some 1,500 denominations and religions. That is why we need, in each succeeding generation, to understand who we are in the light of God's special dealings with us as a people. We are not in the business of proclaiming ourselves better than others, or of pointing a finger at anyone. However, we most definitely are in the business, first of all, of knowing who we are meant to be and, secondly, of obeying God. If He has called us out to be a distinctive people for Him, we cannot risk disobedience. If He wants us to be thoroughly Salvationist, then we are going to be just that. We will persist in bearing the hallmarks of Salvationism, resisting attempts to trivialise or erase them.

The hallmarks I have in mind, distilled after holding Army appointments on five continents and having travelled extensively throughout the Army world, may not be the things often claimed. I am not thinking, for instance, of things like brass bands, ranks, military language or music. We need to go deeper. The lasting marks of Salvationism will not be synonymous with methods, programmes or outward trappings. Usually these are merely a means to an end, though some have, rightly, become dear to us.

A Salvationist cake recipe?

What then is Salvationism? Of what does it consist? Suppose we were about to bake a Salvationist cake. What would be the essential ingredients? Now other cakes might contain some of the same elements, but only a Salvationist cake will have them all. I want to suggest eight ingredients and I will list them first as nouns:

1. *Realism*
2. *Idealism*
3. *Acceptance (or Inclusiveness)*
4. *Compassion*
5. *Simplicity*
6. *Internationalism*
7. *Visibility*
8. *Audibility*

Our cake is going to need all of these blended in equal measure. Let us take each in turn, but now we shall use adjectives instead of nouns, and say: *Salvationism is an expression of the gospel invented by God and entrusted to The Salvation Army. At its best it is realistic, idealistic, accepting, compassionate, simple, international, visible and audible.* It has been in the world now for about 140 years and can be located on every continent in 108 countries.

This description (it is not a definition) calls for explanations. At first sight it may seem a bit bland, as though these are obvious attributes that any church would want to have. So each epithet in the italicised sentence above needs to be unpacked. To this we now turn, because not every denomination would own all of these things. Then at the end I want to add a ninth ingredient called *vulnerability*, because we need to be honest and say out loud to ourselves and to others: *Salvationism is also a vulnerable thing.*

Salvationism is realistic (Distinctive 1)

Salvationism is realistic. It is absolutely down to earth about human nature and sin. They say you can never shock a seasoned Salvationist when describing the depths of your sinful actions or lifestyle. We believe the Bible when it tells us there are no depths to which we cannot sink.

21

We have seen, or actually experienced in our own lives, the true ugliness of sin. Where some might be deterred by this, we are not. We seek divine grace today still to obey the call of yesteryear from our Founder, General William Booth: 'Go for souls and go for the worst souls!' We are called to engage with the lowest. We have to go where they can be found. Salvationism seeks out. It does not sit and wait for the lost to apply for help.

Neither does Salvationism subscribe to the school of thought that sin is OK these days. It is not OK. The Bible says so. Hell will laugh loudly on the day Salvationism fails to uphold boldly, bravely, intelligently and intentionally all godly standards of purity and righteousness. Our grasp of the dreadfulness of sin, of its insidious nature, of its enslaving capacities, is not for weakening. Salvationism is therefore perpetually on its guard. The great Winston Churchill said, 'We must be ready to fend off, at our average moment, whatever the enemy might hurl at us at his selected moment.' He spoke of physical warfare. How much truer then of spiritual warfare!

Salvationism knows that sin is any transgression of the laws or the will of God. It is essentially against God even if the primary victims of our actions are other people. Salvationism sees the sinner as responsible for his own sin, for although likely to sin, people are free agents. We know that sin separates us from God. It involves guilt and attracts divine wrath. It traps and enslaves, darkening the mind and defiling the heart. It weakens the will and dulls the conscience. Its penalty is death, because the sinful and unforgiven soul will not see God. Sin is a terrible evil with dreadful consequences. All this lends urgent wings to our soul-saving work.

However, at the heart of Salvationism is the symbol of the human soul encountering its Redeemer-Creator, the Mercy Seat (Exodus 25:17; 26:34, AV). No Salvation Army place of worship is complete without a Mercy Seat. It is our pulse, our heartbeat. There the sinner finds forgiveness and the saint still further grace. In the midst, therefore, of our realism about sin is a buoyant, unconquerable idealism about the heights to which human beings can rise in Christ.

Salvationism is idealistic (Distinctive 2)

This is not about being naively idealistic. We are not pie-in-the-sky romantics. We have our share of dreamers, but Salvationists dream dreams and see visions in the realm of the achievable. Taking God at his word, we stake everything on the offer of divine forgiveness found in Jesus of Nazareth, Saviour and Son of God. A man or woman can rise from the lowest pits of sin to dwell here and now upon the highest heights of righteousness and purity. Jesus does this for people. Salvationism believes ardently in the availability of divine forgiveness for sins truly repented. We believe, moreover, that this same forgiveness is freely offered to every person. The atonement made by our Lord was made on behalf of the whole of mankind. All who are willing may share in its merciful provision. God has excluded none. He longs for everyone to be saved.

Salvationism thus involves an unquenchable, burning conviction that no person is beyond the love and salvation of God revealed in Jesus Christ. We are to preach, teach and share on all occasions the matchless love of God for sinners. Jesus proved this love at Calvary when He paid the price for our salvation. He took our place. We proclaim the shed blood of Jesus as the only remedy for sin. It is a message that should permeate our preaching, our teaching, our writing, and our thinking at every level. It is the bedrock of every manifestation of Salvationism across the globe.

However, Salvationism will not stop there. We preach the forgiveness of sins, *and* the practical prospect of living a holy life. We are a salvation *and* sanctification Army. In so saying, we have reached a crucial point – some might say the pivotal point – in this essay's analysis of Salvationism.

Idealistic Salvationism and holiness (Distinctive 2 – continued)

We are a holiness people. We must recapture our nerve about the practicality of living a holy life day by day. This book is meant as one more contribution to that process. Explicit, well-informed teaching about sanctification is in danger of becoming a neglected art in our ranks. Yet it is intended by God to be a sacred trust bestowed upon us, a central facet of all we stand for in the world.

Salvationism's Tenth Doctrine affirms: *We believe that it is the privilege of all believers to be wholly sanctified, and that their whole spirit and soul and body may be preserved blameless unto the coming of our Lord Jesus Christ.*

So distinctive is this teaching (few other churches would subscribe to it, the Church of the Nazarene – still numerically significant in North America – being a noted exception) that, along with our position on sacraments (see below), it amounts to just about the only theological stance of special significance that we have been able to offer among the churches. It goes to the very heart of Salvationism. If you will forgive a touch of rhetorical exaggeration, it might even be claimed that Salvationism *is* sanctification, so basic is our Tenth Doctrine to who we are meant to be as a distinct people under God.

A straightforward explanation of Salvationist holiness belief can be found in my *Never the Same Again* (Alexandria, Crest Books, 1997), Chapters 5 and 8. The early 20th century classic writings of Commissioner Samuel Logan Brengle are absolutely seminal, and those of the late Commissioner Edward Read will also enlighten. David Rightmire's *Sanctified Sanity* (Alexandria, Crest Books, 2003) is a most welcome refocus on Brengle's life and teaching. This is to mention only a few of the many helpful literary sources open to every Salvationist. The Army needs its soldiers and officers to be steeped in this key distinctive and to be not only teachers, but also role models, of the holy life. Let our personal holiness be contagious. Let it be 'Christ in you', not something dull or restricting. Let the world see hundreds of thousands of sanctified Salvationists, alive in Christ, filled with the Holy Spirit, victorious daily over sin and temptation in all its forms. Let our lives ring with holy laughter, let our idealism shine forth as we honour the Lord Jesus Christ by the full embracing and realisation of all He has to offer us in this life and beyond.

The theme of the essays in this volume is practical holiness. Each writer sets out to show, in one way or another, that a sanctified life is possible, that it is attractive, relevant, effective, and in fact quite normal. We want to illustrate (as best we can) that there is no aspect of human existence upon which the implications of holiness teaching cannot be brought to bear. It is an everyday thing. It touches the whole of our beings and the whole of life. Salvation deals with past sin. Sanctification deals with, as it were, future sins – the empirical fact that most saved persons continue to sin after conversion.

Let the Army's leaders scour the Territories and Commands all over the world to identify officers and soldiers who know the holiness doctrine, who have grasped it with their minds, who have let their hearts be impacted by it as taught in Scripture, who have grown skilled in explaining it, who can preach it, urge it, counsel it and promote it with undying passion in the language of today. How we need a new generation of sanctified holiness writers and holiness teachers.

With holiness, Salvationism is thus idealistic in the best sense. We believe in the practical ideal of being like Jesus. We are deadly serious about it. We enter into solemn covenants about it when we become soldiers of the Army. We make covenantal promises about our lifestyles and actions. Officers make sacred, lifelong covenants on being commissioned that they will teach and live out the doctrines. Even little Salvationist children are gently encouraged to accept Jesus as Saviour and to promise that they will live 'a life that is clean in thought, word and deed'. If ever there were a pithy, memorable description of a holy life, this is it. If you were ever a Junior Soldier of the Army, go back to your promise card and read it again, this time with the mind and heart of a mature adult, and feel its power, its simple depth. (See Chapter 11 for more on the making of sacred covenants.)

After that, visit Chapter IV of *Chosen to be a Soldier – Orders and Regulations for Soldiers of the Salvation Army* (London, The Salvation Army, 1977, revised 1991) and contemplate the list of eleven 'self-examination' questions drawn up by William Booth. The Founder was of the opinion that there is great gain in a careful self-examination of the soul weekly. He took seriously the teaching of 2 Corinthians 13:5 which contains an exhortation for believers to test themselves. Here are a few samples from Booth's question list:

Am I habitually guilty of any known sin? Do I practise or allow myself in any thought, word or deed which I know to be wrong?

Are my thoughts and feelings such as I should not be ashamed to hear published before God?

Am I doing all in my power for the salvation of sinners? Do I feel concern for their danger?

Am I in danger of being carried away with worldly desire to be rich or admired?

Booth's idealistic Army can thus be seen, when at its best and when being all it is meant to be, as completely and utterly serious about the holy life, though I have no idea how much a list like this is used by Salvationists today. I know some who use it, but I suspect few even know of this help to holiness. As a spiritual exercise it stems from a long tradition found in the teaching and habits of John Wesley who used a not dissimilar list long before Salvationism came on the scene. He and his fellow early Methodists regularly asked themselves 22 holiness health-check questions, such as:

Am I honest in all my acts and words or do I exaggerate?

Did the Bible live in me today?

Am I enjoying prayer?

Am I defeated in any part of my life?

Idealistic? Impossible? Not in Christ and in the power of His love. It is the privilege of all believers, not only Salvationists or Nazarenes, to be wholly sanctified.

Salvationism is accepting / inclusive (Distinctive 3)

Salvationism adopts a stance of arms wide open to others. It is a stance signalling welcome. It is inclusive. Let me mention six short examples of how this works in practice.

First, Salvationism accepts that the gospel is for the whosoever. Nobody is beyond its reach; nobody has sunk too low; nobody has been born destined or predestined to damnation. Our songbook is full to overflowing with songs of invitation to come to the Saviour. The invitation is to everyone.

Second, a stance of acceptance is seen in an absence of snobbery. Salvationism is classless. The universal need of grace, and the knowledge that all have sinned and come short of the glory of God, is a great leveller. Some are better educated, some better off financially, some higher born, but none of this matters to Salvationism. Its focus is on Christ alone, and kneeling before Him we all seek the same Saviour.

Third, Salvationism makes no distinction of gender when it comes to acceptance for ministry opportunities. Nothing is made a male or female preserve. Commissioned officership is open to women and men alike. Married couples are deployed mostly together, and as equals, in ministry appointments. Gender snobbery is banned. So too is academic snobbbery. In testing vocations for full time service as officers, Salvationism does not look primarily at formal educational qualifications (though these are not ignored) but leaves the door wide open for the gifted, Spirit filled, called and committed John or Jane Average who will become key achievers in winning others for Christ. A holy passion for souls, harnessed to a burning hatred of sin, will not be spurned by Salvationism.

Fourth, Salvationism has a sense of humour. Salvationists laugh a lot, often at themselves. We like jokes about our foibles, of which there are plenty. We try not to take ourselves too seriously. Laughter is present in most worship services and this is a healthy sign.

Fifth, Salvationism, while carrying with poise and a measure of self-assurance the distinctives given it by God, is accepting of the place and roles of other church denominations. Salvationism has something to offer at the ecumenical table. It also knows it has something to learn. The sharing of insights is a two way process. (For a formal statement on The Salvation Army in relation to other churches, see the Appendix at the end of this Chapter.)

Sixth and last, mention should be made of Salvationism's accepting attitude to those of other faiths. We long for their conversion to Christ, but we will respect their beliefs and, in accordance with the wise counsel of the Founder, never offer criticism. Instead Salvationism prefers a quiet, positive, courteous word of personal witness when the opportunity arises.

Salvationism is compassionate (Distinctive 4)

Today everyone who knows the Army expects Salvationism to manifest itself with a face of compassion. Salvationism is the friend of the poor. It is biased toward the social underdog. Compassionate Salvationism is aligned with need, so much so that according to one famous, but supportive, TV journalist here in New Zealand, Salvationists 'have the smell of the streets' on them. This was said as an enormous compliment. It struck home.

The public has high expectations which can be fulfilled by the Army only in the power of Christ. A classless Army, we follow our working class, carpenter Saviour, whose hands were smeared and worn with manual toil, whose finger nails were not always clean, and whose disciples too knew the meaning of sweat and labour. We get our hands dirty if need be among the downtrodden and vulnerable. Some have seen Salvationism as 'Christianity with its sleeves rolled up'. There is much to live up to.

Salvationism has been endowed by God with a marked giftedness and capacity to love the loveless and to serve the outcast. It represents so huge a burden of responsibility that we tremble at the thought.

Compassionate Salvationism's tool kit comprises the basin and the towel, both literally and metaphorically. Feet get washed and spirits healed through programmes for: addictions, homelessness, domestic violence, broken families, abandoned children, illiteracy, health education, income generation, job training, food parcel distribution – the list seems endless. It is all sustained in being by God. He garners the resources. He provides the drive, the energy to keep going. Sometimes He takes us by surprise and opens up the way for innovative, imaginative expressions of compassionate action. In the city of Christchurch, New Zealand, God is working out his purposes through a Salvation Army boxing club and, more recently, through a tattoo removal program, something especially meaningful to new converts whose tattoos can feel like seemingly unbreakable bonds with an unregenerate past.

Salvationism is simple (Distinctive 5)

Salvationism is essentially simple. In this context I am using 'simple' to mean uncomplicated, or not complex. Simplicity ought not to be confused with superficiality. Salvationism has depth, but seeks to avoid complications.

This is seen in our worship styles. We adopt no complicated liturgy, no set forms. Directness is the key; spontaneity the spirit. Preparation is crucial, but plans can be instantly changed or abandoned altogether if God's Spirit so leads. Preaching is meant to be simple – over nobody's head – but deep enough to appeal to the most thoughtful person present. Meetings and worship events mount steadily to a moment of simple choice: for Christ or not; for sanctification or not. The goals are simple: first to honour God, and then to bring out in the attendee a verdict, a response in the heart. The inspiration is the pattern set by Jesus in telling his parables, each calling forth a watershed response on the part of the hearer. Simple, yet deep.

Salvationism's simplicity is found also in Salvationist ceremonies. Each one – the dedication of children, weddings, funerals, the making of new soldiers, and so on – is intentionally simple, avoiding frills.

The aim is dignity with accessibility. No mystery for its own sake. No hype just for effect. No complexities or grandness that could ever lead the participant mistakenly to think it is the ceremony that imparts grace, requiring no faith in the heart.

Very close to this is the simple, thought-through absence of sacraments. Salvationism rejoices in a God-given liberty from sacramental ritual. Instead it embraces a simple belief in, and world-wide witness to, the immediacy of divine grace. Salvationists have been spared the tortuous, divisive disputations found wherever sacraments are debated and made central. We need take no sides in the age-old tensions about format and theology. We can simply look on in slight, but always benign, bewilderment as others, all sincerely intent on obeying what may never have been commanded, follow widely different rituals based on endless varieties of theologies while claiming authenticity for their own 'this' over someone else's 'that'. In its simplicity, Salvationism stands called out by God to show in daily living the viability of holiness and Christly compassion free from sacraments or anything that might be mistakenly understood to be a sacrament. (See further *Who Are These Salvationists?*, Part II – Chapters 4,5,6.)

Salvationism's formal Doctrines are also simple, pared down statements of belief. The eleven Articles of Faith are all short and pithy. The language is almost monosyllabic, the content consistent with mainstream, orthodox Protestantism. The *Handbook of Doctrine* in each edition (the 1940 edition is especially powerful) manages an exposition that can be grasped by simple, straightforward folk. It is profound stuff, handling revealed truth in language that is accessible and in a style that does not threaten. Simple Salvationism.

Salvationism is international (Distinctive 6)

In saying that Salvationism is international we mean much more than that The Salvation Army can be found in a large number of countries. Salvationist internationalism is about holding all people as brothers and sisters under one Heavenly Father, the Creator of all. Salvationism sees no race, no ethnic group, no skin colour, and no culture as superior to another. It affirms natural feelings of patriotism, proper pride in one's own country and its achievements, but eschews nationalism with its overtones of racial superiority.

Salvationism teaches that Christians are citizens of the world before they are citizens of their own countries. 'All lands,' said General Bramwell Booth, 'are my fatherland, for all lands are my Father's.' God has given us the whole globe as our arena, and therefore we can regard no person as our enemy, even in time of war. Salvationism is as serious as that about being international.

Salvationism is visible (Distinctive 7)

Invisible Salvationism is a contradiction in terms. Salvationism seeks everywhere a high profile in order to be seen and heard. The impetus for this is sometimes to attract funding for social programmes. A better reason is to draw attention to the claims of Christ. With a highly visible profile we can, as it were, punch beyond our weight. We can impact for God far beyond our numerical strength.

Salvationism wears a uniform for two reasons: as a witness to Christ, and as a means of announcing one's availability to others. Salvationism lives for others. It longs for others to be saved, and cannot rest while others are in need. Only those committing to soldiership in the Army are entitled to don the uniform, but soldiers have a choice. The uniform is not mandatory. However, we need more wearing it than not wearing it if we are to remain visible. It has always seemed to me a worthy motive for becoming a soldier of the Army, namely the chance to wear the uniform and be seen to be Christ's person. Visibility is a sacred privilege. Salvationism does not take it lightly.

Salvationism is audible (Distinctive 8)

Mention of audible Salvationism will attract wisecracks about loud brass bands and rattling tambourines. That is OK. It is a great experience to hear Army musicians and congregations raise the roof in praise of God. There is, however, something else to be said. If invisible Salvationism is a contradiction in terms, so too is silent Salvationism. We must make our message heard. This is true of the gospel message for the unsaved. Nothing could be more urgent, more important. Some of you reading this will want to 'leave your nets' to become available in the Army for full time service. You can spend your whole life, devote all your energies to making the Good News of Christ audible.

There is, however, another aspect to Salvationist audibility. We have already looked at compassionate Salvationism and the addressing of human need. Compassionate Salvationism is not complete unless it is also an audible Salvationism. Salvationism is a voice for the voiceless. It is willing to take risks to be heard on behalf of those who cannot speak. This is a natural consequence of being biased toward the poor.

Need gets revealed in symptoms, yet there never was a symptom that had no cause. Audible, intelligent Salvationism can never be satisfied with dealing only with symptoms. It is the causes of need which cry out for attention. *Why* are children hungry? *Why* are women battered? *Why* are food parcels still needed in rich countries in the 21st century?

Advocacy in the public arena on the causes of social deprivation is a demanding pursuit. There are those who will warn us off, citing possible loss of financial support if we upset some by being truthfully and penetratingly audible. That will not do. Salvationism that ducks the issue is no Salvationism. We are called as much to social action as we are to social service.

Salvationism will be heard. Salvationism needs to show up in the debating chambers of the nation, in the halls of influence, in the TV studio and radio station. Salvationism has world-formative things to say and dare not, cannot be silent. When Salvationism speaks, it speaks for Christ. The price of silence is unthinkable.

This brings us now to that additional, final characteristic of Salvationism, vulnerability.

Modern Salvationism is vulnerable

Modern Salvationism is vulnerable in ways that have crept up on us sometimes unperceived.

In seeking to set down eight key, distinctive elements (I have called them non-negotiables) of Salvationism I have intentionally written about Salvationism at its best, as though it were always and everywhere just so. Now, of course, things are not quite like that. Today Salvationism is vulnerable. In the final part of this essay, let us examine this.

Already we have said that God invented Salvationism, but handed it over to folk now called Salvationists. That was a divine risk. God knew what he was doing when he gave it all to *flawed human beings*. I cannot think of any religious body that would not say the same of itself. So Salvationism, on a human level, is in the hands of far from perfect mortals. These are constantly in need of more grace, regularly seeking forgiveness.

Though the Army is growing globally, it is experiencing *damaging numerical losses* in too many places. This has been happening for quite some time. Growth in Africa and South Asia is tremendous, but not in Europe or in the western, English-speaking democracies. In the land where Salvationism was born, the United Kingdom, losses in numbers of Army soldiers are very high year after year. Child conversions are also less frequent. Some corps officers in places I have visited around the globe seem no longer to know how to lead a child to Christ. We are seeing a new phenomenon: Army corps that have no Junior Soldiers at all. This neglect will return to haunt us.

Vulnerability is seen also in *uncertainty about our identity* and mission in recent years. Not all Salvationists can articulate just who we are meant to be under God. There has been some loss of nerve, with waning confidence in Salvationism's distinctives, the very things this essay is about. This has shown itself in occasional attempts to water down the essentials of Salvationism, and to retreat from the beauty and ongoing relevance of soldiership in the Army. Some corps have tried to become pale reflections of other evangelical churches, to our lasting detriment. We are witnessing here and there a lack of poise, a diminution of the conviction that God invented Salvationism and that *God raised up* the Army. Once these truths are recaptured, recovery might begin in those places where it is needed.

Salvationism is vulnerable to *financial pressures*. So vast is the social programming, so costly the endeavour, that we are forever in need of money. Vulnerability arises when we start to trim our Salvationist sails to the winds of the world and the dollar. We cannot always expect to be popular. Jesus was not. The apostles were not. William Booth was not. Today, however, mostly we are. Why is that?

The ongoing *secularisation of our employee force* is another potentially disastrous source of vulnerability. The genius of Salvationism has from the outset been that its mission is carried out by saved persons. Each employee was to be a partner in mission. Although we have many fine Christians on staff, this basic concept has all but been abandoned. Salvationism has been left vulnerable.

Threats are arising also from a growing *uncertainty about officership*. Roles once carried out only by called, trained, covenanted-for-life officers today might be found being performed by lay employees, not all of whom, as already noted, are committed Christians. The morale of officers is at risk. The attractiveness of officership is in danger of being affected in proportion to its distinctiveness being undermined. Vulnerability thus arises from the blurring of lines between the functions of ordained and commissioned officers, and roles assigned to others willing to serve as lay Salvationists or as employees. There are many parts of the Army world where these things need to be quickly addressed. It is not too alarmist to say that in some lands officership is at risk. The risk deepens wherever those who have made a lifelong vocational covenant are marginalised in favour of those whose intentions are explicitly short term or transitory.

The greatest threat of all today for Salvationism is a perceptible *neglect of holiness teaching*. Left unchecked, this has the potential to undermine Salvationism right at its very heart. We are less surefooted about it than once we were. William Booth used to say that there are few subjects of which we more frequently speak, or in which we more truly glory, than that of holiness of heart and life. Is this still so? No, it is not. Some among us, well-meaning but misguided, seek to offer the substitute of pseudo-sacraments or imitation sacraments for solid, Bible-based teaching on, and seeking after, the holy life. The blessing of a clean heart is no longer spoken about or witnessed to. Many (most?) Salvationists today would simply not know what we mean by the phrase, 'the blessing of a clean heart'.

God, who raised us up, is calling us to be open and honest about the present state of Salvationism in the world. This same God, however, is good and there are remarkable things being accomplished by His power. The commitment and work rate of Salvation Army officers and staff that I have met on five continents is impressive to say the least. We can recognise that the Army is still fruitful for God, in whose holy heart there once arose an emotion so strong that Salvationism was born.

From the heart of God we came. In the hands of God we are held. In the strength of God we trust. He will bless us as an Army if we remain true to our first calling. Paradoxically, it is largely the old wells that beckon us into the future.

(For insights on the further Salvationist distinctive of 'covenant' see Chapter 11 by Captain Stephen Court.)

Appendix

The following statement has been published and used for official purposes by The Salvation Army in the United Kingdom and in New Zealand, Fiji and Tonga.

The Salvation Army in Relation to Other Christian Denominations

A Position Statement
(by Shaw Clifton)

See *Reflections – How Churches View Their Life and Mission* (London, BCC, 1986)

Summary Statement

1. The church universal comprises all true believers in Jesus Christ.

2. Believers stand in a spiritual relationship to one another which is not dependent upon any particular church structure.

3. The Salvation Army is part of the church universal and a Christian denomination called into and sustained in being by God.

4. Denominational variety is not self-evidently contrary to God's will for His people.

5. Inter-denominational harmony and co-operation are valuable for the enriching of the life and witness of each denomination.

6. The Salvation Army seeks and welcomes inter-church and ecumenical involvement in the 108 countries where the Army is present.

Amplified Statement

The Church Universal

1. WE BELIEVE that the church, the body of Christ (Ephesians 1:23), comprises all who are born not of blood, nor of the will of the flesh, nor of the will of man, but of God (John 1:13). The church universal includes all who believe in the Lord Jesus Christ and confess Him as Lord.

WE DO NOT BELIEVE that the church universal depends for its existence or validity upon any particular ecclesiastical structure, any particular form of worship, or any particular observance of ritual.

2. WE BELIEVE that the church universal is the whole of the worshipping, witnessing Christian community throughout the centuries into whatever groupings, large or small, accepted or persecuted, wealthy or poor, her members may have been structured in the past or are governed in the present.

WE DO NOT BELIEVE that an adequate definition of the church can be confined in terms of ecclesiastical structure, but must rather be stated in terms of a spiritual relationship. Members of the church are those who are incorporated into Christ Jesus (Ephesians 1:1) and therefore reconciled to God through His Son. All such are in a spiritual relationship one with the other which begins and continues regardless of externals, according to the prayer of Jesus that those who are His may be one (John 17:23). These words of Jesus ask for a oneness as is found in the oneness of Father and Son. This oneness is spiritual, not organisational.

3. WE BELIEVE that The Salvation Army is part of the church universal and a representative of the body of Christ. Christ is the True Vine (John 15:1) and believers are His living, fruit-bearing branches.

WE DO NOT BELIEVE that any community of true followers of Christ can rightly be regarded as outside the church universal, whatever their history, customs or practices when set in comparison with those of other Christian communities. God alone knows those who are truly His (2 Timothy 2:19).

Denominational Variety

4. WE BELIEVE that God's dealings with His people are perfect according to His will, but that human responses are imperfect and prone to error. It may be God's dealings or fallible human responses to those dealings which have brought about the rich and varied denominational tapestry discernible today.

WE DO NOT BELIEVE that denominational or organisational variety can automatically and in every case be said to be contrary to God's will for His people.

5. WE BELIEVE that God raised up The Salvation Army and inspired the distinctives of Salvationism according to His purposes for His glory and the proclamation of the gospel.

WE DO NOT BELIEVE that The Salvation Army's existence as an independent and distinctive Christian community, having no formal, structural ties with other Christian communities, is an affront to the gospel of Jesus Christ or self-evidently contrary to God's will for the whole of His body on earth.

6. WE BELIEVE that the practices of The Salvation Army have much in common with the practices of other churches, but that being raised up by God for a special work, the Army has been led to adopt the following distinctive combination of characteristics:

a) its emphasis upon personal religion and individual spiritual regeneration through faith in Christ, leading in turn to a commitment to seek to win others to Christ;
b) its teaching concerning holy living;
c) its insistence that the gospel is for the whosoever;
d) its use of the Mercy Seat;
e) its avoidance of set forms in worship, seeking to encourage spontaneity;
f) its teaching that the receiving of inward spiritual grace is not dependent upon any particular outward observance;
g) its requirement that full members (Soldiers) publicly confess their faith in Jesus Christ as their Saviour and Lord, and enter into a formal doctrinal and ethical commitment, the latter including abstention from alcohol, tobacco, and non-medical use of addictive drugs;

h) its encouragement into Army fellowship of those unable to enter into the formal commitment of Soldiership;

i) its strong commitment to evangelism, including outdoor evangelism;

j) its witness through the wearing of distinctive uniform on the part of most Salvationists;

k) its recognition of the equal place of women and men in all aspects of Christian ministry and leadership;

l) its vocation under God to serve the needy and to be a voice for the voiceless;

m) its world-wide structure and its emphasis upon internationalism;

n) its freedom from, and intentional non-use of, sacramental practices.

These are part of the blessings which have come through God's gracious dealings with us through the years.

WE DO NOT BELIEVE it to be self-evidently God's will for His people in the Army that they cast aside in haste the blessings of the years.

The Local Church

7. WE BELIEVE that just as the true church universal comprises all who believe on the Lord Jesus Christ, so each denominational church comprises a community of true believers who have in common the way the Lord, through His Holy Spirit, has dealt with them as a community. In turn, each denominational church comprises local churches regularly meeting together for worship, fellowship and service in a relatively confined geographical location.

WE DO NOT BELIEVE that the validity of a denomination or its local churches depends upon any particular ecclesiastical tradition, structure, hierarchy, form of worship, or ritual. Where even two or three gather in

Christ's name there He is present (Matthew 18:20) with a presence no less real than that discerned in larger, more formal or ritualistic settings.

The Army's Identity

8. WE BELIEVE that The Salvation Army is an international evangelical Christian denomination with other Christian denominations and that the Army's local corps are local churches with the local churches of other denominations. The Army springs from the Methodist revival and has remained unassimilated by any other denomination.

WE DO NOT BELIEVE that The Salvation Army's history, structures, practices or beliefs permit it to be understood as anything other than a distinct Christian denomination with a purpose to fulfil and a calling to discharge under God. Similarly, its local corps cannot properly be understood unless seen primarily as local churches meeting regularly in Christ's name for worship, fellowship and service. Commissioned officers (both men and women) of The Salvation Army are ordained ministers of the Christian gospel, called by God and empowered by the Holy Spirit to preach and teach apostolic truth in the name of Christ and for His sake.

The Army and other Churches

9. WE BELIEVE that it is God's will that harmonious ecumenical relations are built up and sustained, by His grace, between Christians everywhere and between all Christian denominations including their local churches. The Army's numerous and widespread contacts with other Christian communities both in Britain and around the world serve to enrich the Army's spirituality and to enhance its understanding of the work of the Spirit. For this reason the Army welcomes such contacts and seeks cordially to extend and deepen them.

WE DO NOT BELIEVE that narrowness or exclusiveness are consistent with God's will for His people, or that God has nothing to teach us by

our sharing and co-operating with His people in other denominations.
10. WE BELIEVE that every visible unit of the Church universal is
endowed with its own blessings and strengths as gifts from God. We
respect, and in many cases admire, those strengths recognising too that
because of human frailty every denomination, including The Salvation
Army, has its imperfections.

WE DO NOT BELIEVE it is our task or place to criticise or undermine
the traditions or emphases of other denominations, and certainly not
in relation to the sacraments on which our stance is unusual, though
not unique. It is contrary to our practices to offer hostile comment upon
the life of any denomination or local church. We are anxious not to
denigrate the doctrines or practices of any other Christian group. The
Army places emphasis in its teaching not upon externals but upon the
need for each believer personally to experience that inward spiritual grace
to which the external observance testifies. We maintain that no external
observance can rightly be said to be essential to salvation and that the
biblical truth is that we can meet with God and receive His grace
anywhere at any time.

11. WE BELIEVE The Salvation Army was called into being by the will of
God, is sustained in being by God's grace, and is empowered for
obedience by the Holy Spirit. Its overriding purpose is to win the souls
of men and women and boys and girls for God, whilst working
simultaneously, and for Christ's sake, to alleviate the material lot of
those in need.

WE DO NOT BELIEVE that we alone are called to this sacred and
awesome task and therefore we rejoice that in other Christian churches
we find co-workers for God.

CHAPTER 2

NEW LOVE

HOLINESS AND THE ELEVENTH COMMANDMENT

THERE exists an absolutely basic question for every Christian. It is this: 'Is there a way of behaving, a form of conduct, a personal lifestyle that only Christians can engage in and which would therefore be impossible for a non-Christian?'

It is equally a key question for every unbeliever: 'Is there behaviour which an unsaved person is incapable of undertaking, and which is thus the exclusive prerogative of a follower of Jesus?'

The issue has always been there, but is especially important today when we are being told that tolerance is king and that we should not place emphasis on the differences between faiths, or even on the difference between faith and atheism. If we were to believe this, evangelical efforts would cease and we would be guilty of betraying the mission imperative of the Lord when He told us to go into all the world and make disciples.

The recent rise and ongoing widening influence of Islam in western democracies heightens the importance of knowing our faith. The United Kingdom now has more Moslems than Methodists. Moslem numbers are escalating in the USA and in all western countries. Hence the need to be able to live out and to explain intelligently the practical daily difference our religion makes to us and the plus it gives to our personal conduct.

This was brought home to me when serving in the Islamic Republic of Pakistan. There we needed to be able to show clear blue water between the three million of us who were Christians and the 140 million Islamic majority who rejected Christ as Saviour. Our own Salvationists asked to be taught the real, down to earth difference between their faith and that of Islam, not only in belief and doctrine, not just in the histories of the two faiths, but the difference in daily, hourly living. Crucially, *this* difference (among many differences) is to be discovered in Salvationist teaching on the holy life built upon the love of Jesus. Hence the title of this Chapter.

So, back now to the original question. Is it worthwhile being a Christian? Does following Jesus actually work? Is there a practical outcome in which the unbeliever cannot share? For an answer we must

43

turn to the Scriptures. Three passages offer themselves as candidates in the quest for the answer.

The 'Great Commandment' (Mark 12:29-31)

The famous words of Jesus, 'Love your neighbour as yourself', have come to be known as the Great Commandment. They place an ethical demand upon us. They have a place in how the holy life is to be lived day by day. Our dealings with all we meet are to be governed by this imperative.

So can this be the answer to the question raised at the beginning of this Chapter? Is 'love of neighbour' the exclusive domain of Christians? Can only a saved person obey this saying? Is this the pinnacle of the ethical teaching of Jesus?

An examination of the context in which the words were spoken will help. First, this is said as part of a conversation with a Jewish sect called Sadducees. It is about a point of Jewish religious law. It is spoken in reply to a question put to Jesus by a Jewish religious lawyer, a scribe (NIV: 'one of the teachers of the law', verse 28). In His reply Jesus is summarising the whole of the Jewish religious law code given through Moses. It is all very Jewish!

Here Jesus is stating in a nutshell the essence of the Jewish religious ethic, rather than that of what we would now call the Christian ethic. In other words a good, observing Jew can obey the Great Commandment. You do not necessarily have to be a Christian in order to love your neighbour as yourself (though it surely does help). Moreover, some of us love ourselves with a modest measure of self-love, thus rendering the demand in turn a modest one.

So the Great Commandment seems not to be the answer to our initial question, even though it is a famous, memorable, penetrating saying of Jesus. While it is not the *heart* of His ethical teaching for us, we need to note clearly that it is indeed *part* of what He has to say to us and we cannot ignore it. If a pious non-Christian can obey it, then how much more ought we also to fulfil it. A life in disobedience to this command is not a holy life. However, we note that there is more, much more, something higher yet for those who are made over anew in Christ.

We turn therefore to another renowned moral exhortation from the lips of the Lord.

The 'Golden Rule' (Luke 6:31)

The NIV puts the Golden Rule like this: 'Do to others as you would have them do to you.' In common parlance this has become the proverb: 'Do as you would be done by.' Is this the answer to our question? Is it the high point of Christian moral teaching? Can only followers of Jesus obey it?

Note that Jesus was not the first to say this. The famous Chinese teacher and philosopher, Confucius, five centuries before Jesus was born said the same thing but stated it in the negative: 'Do not do to others what you do not want them to do to you.' Jesus took this and rendered it in fresh, positive terms. We need only look around us to see that many live like this. Not all of them are Christians. Some are good Jews or good Hindus (as was Gandhi), and some are simply reasonably decent pagans – atheists or agnostics.

Happily many of those living in obedience to the Golden Rule are also Christians, even though it is not the highest teaching the Lord has for us. Again we need to regard it as *part* of his demand on us, but not the *heart* of it. We are to live in holy conformity with it, but again there is more, much more.

Let us go on searching the Scriptures by moving into the Fourth Gospel.

The 'New Commandment' (John 13:34)

On the eve of His execution, knowing time was short, Jesus told the disciples in the Upper Room: 'A new command I give you: Love one another. As I have loved you, so you must love one another.' These sublime words are known as the New Commandment. In John 15:12 we hear the echo: 'My command is this: Love each other as I have loved you.'

Two words leap from the pages of the Bible as we ponder this: 'command' and 'new'. Jesus is making two claims. First He is implying beyond all doubt that He is divine, for only God can give the human race commandments. The Ten Commandments came directly from God through Moses. Now here is the Son of God establishing an Eleventh Commandment, as authoritative and as binding as the first Ten. Next He is declaring that what He is about to say has never, in all of history, been said before. It is new.

You will no doubt have seen, when browsing in Christian book stores, devotional trinkets that have on them the words: 'Love one another.' These words are not enough. They truncate the command. The New Commandment has two clauses: 1) love one another; 2) as I have loved you. To omit the second clause is to rob the command of its meaning.

This New Commandment is the answer to the original question with which we began. It has staggering implications. It calls us to holiness of action and of relationship not only in response to the example of Jesus, but to an obedience built upon an infusion into our lives of the divine and sacred love Jesus offered to all He met and offers still. The Eleventh Commandment is not only a command to love; it is an invitation to be filled with the love of Christ, again and again. It is an offer of new love.

If you have not opened your heart and life to this offer and if you have not accepted the love of Christ – in other words, if you are not a Christian – you cannot obey this command. No faith, then no new love. No acceptance of Christ, then no capacity to obey His words. Only those born again in Christ can do it. Commissioner Samuel Logan Brengle, that great prophet of holiness, taught that the baptism of the Holy Spirit was a baptism of love. He was right. The holy life is a life lived in regular, spontaneous obedience to the New Commandment. The holy life is a life of new love, Christ-like love.

Even the lawyers know that you cannot give what you do not have. The legal world has a way of putting its key principles of justice and procedure into pithy Latin sayings. One such is: *'Nemo dat quod non habet'* or 'You cannot give what you do not have.' It refers usually to the passing of a valid title to property. For example, if you do not own the house you cannot pass on a valid ownership to anyone else. So it is with the love of Christ. If you have not accepted it, you cannot share or show it. Only true disciples of Jesus are able to obey John 13:34, and obedience to this New Commandment is a valid test of the authenticity of a life said to be holy.

The New Commandment is thus the pinnacle of Christian ethics. It goes to the heart of all conduct claiming to be worthy of the label 'Christian'. It is Jesus' highest moral command upon us, and with it comes an offer of Himself to indwell and enable. No Moslem, no Jew, no Buddhist, no Hindu, no atheist, no agnostic can obey the command of the Lord in this, unless there is a coming to Christ and an accepting of His forgiveness and love as our Saviour from sin.

This raises a final and highly significant question. Can even Christians truly obey this New Commandment?

Is it possible to obey John 13:34?

If we are candid we will acknowledge that not all Christians live in obedience to the New Commandment. Many of us fall short. The sin of lovelessness, sadly, is not a rare thing within the Body of Christ.

What is this love we are invited to receive and share? The Greek of the New Testament calls it *agape*. This is the word used in the Bible every time the love of God for us is mentioned. It is the word used in John 13:34 and 15:12. The Greek language had two other words for love. One was *eros* and referred to the love between a woman and a man, as in the love shared between spouses. Another was *philia* to denote the love that springs up between parent and child or between brother and sister. Sexual (or erotic) love and family (or friendship) love usually cannot survive unless returned. The love of God shown in Christ, *agape* love, is different, however. It goes on loving though not returned. It does not die in the face of rejection. Though spurned, it does not spurn. It enriches and transforms *eros* and *philia*. (See Chapter 3, 'Three Ways of Loving', for more on these themes.)

It is this love, the unique, enduring, eternal love of God that is held out to us in the New Commandment. 'Here it is,' says the Lord. 'Take me. Receive me. Let me fill you with my love, then pour it out, pour me out, for others through a holy life lived in the power of my indwelling you.'

Can it be? Does it happen? Yes. The days of being Spirit-filled are not over. Holiness of life has not had its day. The Lord holds out His offer yet to all ready to receive Him in fullness. Imagine every Salvationist filled to overflowing with the love of Christ. Capture a vision of every Salvationist – officers and soldiers alike – on their knees before God pleading for a life in obedience to new love. For that is how it happens. We have all known since we were little children how to get what we wanted: we went to our Mum or Dad and asked for it. It is the same in this matter of the soul.

John 14:13, 14 are key verses. Here we find the Lord Jesus making yet another divine promise: 'I will do whatever you ask in my name, so that the Son may bring glory to the Father. You may ask me for anything in my name and I will do it.' So it would seem that obedience to the New Commandment begins on our knees, at the altar, asking to be infilled, indwelt by the living Christ who loves us and has died for us. To get it you must ask. Ask now. Ask here. God does not invade us uninvited. Neither does He toy with us. He never makes demands on us and then abandons us. With each demand comes grace. When He commands, He empowers.

To be like Jesus!
This hope possesses me,
In every thought and deed,
This is my aim, my creed;
To be like Jesus!
This hope possesses me,
His Spirit helping me,
Like him I'll be.
(John Gowans)

CHAPTER 3

THREE WAYS OF LOVING

HOLINESS AND INTERPERSONAL RELATIONSHIPS

LOVE is an overused word. It is used so glibly these days. 'I love you', said to a spouse or parent, is not the same as 'I love chocolate'. 'I love going to the movies' is not the same as 'I love God'. So the three distinctions made in the Greek language (mentioned in the last Chapter) are a very helpful basis for sorting out the different meanings of 'love'. This in turn deepens our understanding of what is means to live a holy, sanctified life.

According to the Greeks, love in the family was *philia*. Love between a man and a woman was *eros*. In the Greek New Testament love from heaven, the love of God revealed perfectly in Jesus (I shall call it heaven-love), was *agape* (pronounced 'aga-pay'). The Greek words denote three ways of loving. Each is special, each is distinct, but all three are related. Love is at the heart of holiness. The blessing of a clean heart is a baptism of love. A Christian cannot speak of holiness and not mention love. Conversely we ought not to speak of love without recognising its central place in the holy life. Such a life is one modelled upon Jesus Christ, the epitome of love revealed.

Love in the family – philia

Some years ago a family life conference was held in Japan. It lasted two weeks and in that time the delegates could not move beyond discussing a definition of 'family'. No agreement was reached. Christians know that according to the plan of God for the world a family is something that begins with a wedding. It is grounded in marriage. A man and a woman might physically leave their own families, without ceasing to belong to them as kith and kin, and they marry, becoming one flesh (Genesis 2:24). This is the origin of a new family unit, with connections reaching out in all directions to the extended family.

These days everybody knows that not all unions are marked by marriage (see below and also Chapter 6). Some men and women, especially in the western democracies, cohabit without marriage and bring children into the world and see themselves as a family. So too do some intentionally single parents. Even people who embark on same sex relationships claim they have thereby formed a new family. None of this accords with the Biblical norm. However, we cannot ignore it. It is modern reality. Salvationists want to continue to see family as rooted in marriage, without rejecting or alienating others who opt for informal liaisons. We also want to share sensitively the need for all 'family' relationships to be brought under the Lordship of Christ. All expressions of *philia* can be placed at the feet of Jesus, resulting in transformation.

It was Billy Graham who said that a nation is only as strong as its homes. Homes are full of people of different ages and personalities. Let us look at a portion of Scripture that gives crystal clear guidance. It is Titus 2:1-14. There is something here for everyone in the family: older men, older women, younger women and young men. The counsel in Titus was intended for those within the church, but it can apply to those within the family too.

Older men

For a man to be mature he needs to be temperate, not given to excesses. Sometimes Titus 2:2 is taken to mean sober, or serious. A father or grandfather is not meant to be a flippant or superficial person. He owes it to the rest of the family to have gravitas when it is required. He will be called upon for advice and to take the lead in the family. He must therefore be worthy of respect. Respect needs to be earned. It can be lost. An older man devoted to Christ will become worthy by the grace of Christ. He will be indwelt by Christ. Others will see in him that fruit of the Holy Spirit known as self-control (see Galatians 5:22). He will be sound in faith, so that his family realise he is leaning on God daily. He will be sound in love, *agape* love, because he has received the love of Christ. He will be sound in endurance, never giving up on his loved ones or losing ultimate patience with them. All this is a pen portrait of a sanctified older man. It is family love (*philia*) embodied in holiness.

Older women

A Christian mother or grandmother needs to have a reverent lifestyle, one that reveres God. She will have gained control over her tongue, eschewing gossip and slander. She will have learned that the more you say the more likely you are to sin. A godly older woman will keep herself busy so that there is no time for the boredom that can lead to a desire for damaging stimulants like alcohol or drugs. Imagine her children or grandchildren finding her intoxicated! She will find herself being looked to for guidance and teaching on all sorts of matters, from kitchen recipes through spiritual help to boyfriend / girlfriend problems. The younger married women will need someone like her to look up to. Once more we see a pen portrait of a sanctified older woman, a further instance of *philia* embodied in holiness.

Younger women

A sensible younger woman will be ready to learn from those who are older and wiser, not least when it comes to devotion to a husband or to children. Marriage and parenthood involve learned skills, which in a mature character are known collectively as wisdom. This is handed down from generation to generation. A young Christian woman is intended by God to be sexually pure, whether single or married. If single, she will be celibate; if married, faithful. This will call for self-control, that same essential fruit of the Holy Spirit mentioned earlier. For a believer, self-control comes from God-control. Such a young woman will never let her words or actions, whether in the home or beyond, bring the gospel into disrepute. If she is married, her relationship with her husband, both in public and in private will be in accordance with the Scriptures. All this adds up to a portrait of a sanctified young woman. It is again *philia* expressed in holiness.

Young men

Titus 2:6 places self-control again high on the agenda, this time for a Christian young man. It seems to be basic to a Christ-like personality. How vital that young men, with their youthful impetuosity and strong natural appetites, bring all they have and are to Christ. They can accomplish amazing things despite their lack of years or experience if only they will submit to Christ. They can bring goodness into other lives, and even become teachers of the faith. They will come to have a reputation for being true to their word. A Christian young man's conversation will not be loaded with dubious double meanings. He will find plenty to laugh about without that. God will use him in such a way that the reputation of the gospel will be enhanced. In short, a young man can be a living example of sanctified *philia*. He will be a credit to his family and stand tall among his friends.

A further word to the middle-aged
The fifth Commandment (Exodus 20:12) was written especially for the middle-aged. Too often we have assumed it is for little children: 'Honour your father and your mother...' How many times have parents quoted this to their minor offspring? It is a Command about *philia* love. Grown up, middle-aged children need to hear it. Each of the Ten Commandments was originally meant for the nomadic Israelites. They were laws for adults to obey and to then pass on to their children. Meanwhile, it is middle-aged children who are to honour their elderly parents if they want to inherit the promise attached to the Command. How ought a sanctified middle-aged person treat a parent? By never visiting them? By unthinkingly assuming that someone else will look after them? No. Instead, an elderly parent is to honoured, esteemed, written to, visited, listened to, heeded, still obeyed if need be, brought into the family circle and respected for being the oldest, most experienced and probably the wisest person there. This is *philia* at its best.

Nothing new under the sun
Family life has not changed that much through the centuries. The Bible's teaching for *philia* relationships is as needed, as powerful and as relevant today as it was for the first believers. The problems have always been there. 'We are seeing the decay of good family life; parental control is a thing of the past and children no longer obey their parents.' Who said this? It might have been any of us alive today. However, these words were found by archaeologists in Egypt and written on a slab of stone 3000 years old!

Again: 'The world is passing through troublous times. The young people of today think of nothing but themselves. They have no reverence for parents or old age. They talk as if they knew everything. As for the girls, they are forward and immodest.' Is this from a modern magazine or newspaper, or from a sermon preached recently? No! They are the words of Peter the Hermit in 1274!

Love in the family has never been an easy thing. Some of our strongest temptations and greatest failures have been in the setting of family life. *Philia* is the love or affection shared between family members or in deep friendships. When transformed by the love of Christ (*agape*) it becomes a key ingredient of the holy life.

Love between a man and a woman – eros

The famous traffic intersection in the heart of downtown London, England known as Piccadilly Circus has at its centre a statue of Eros, a mythical winged messenger of the (even more) mythical gods. Eros was reputed to shoot arrows into the hearts of humans so that they become love-struck. The statue's name is taken from *eros*, Greek for sexual love, and the root for other English words like 'erotic' or 'eroticism'.

Sexuality and sexual love are part of God's plan for the human race. Love between a man and a woman has a place of profound meaning in God's grand scheme of things. It is important to say this at the outset because the Christian church has not always seen it that way. Sex and sexuality were once regarded as necessary evils. They proved useful for procreating the species, but were not for indulgence or to be celebrated. It was simply not done to speak of pleasure in sex.

New insights now prevail. Our bodies are designed by God and are a marvel of divine creativity (whatever their shape!). Our natural, normal sexual appetites are God-given. They are part of God's creation and therefore good. God looked upon everything He had made and called it 'very good' (Genesis 1:31). He created us and then lovingly set parameters for us. We can use our created drives and impulses in accordance with His will or not. We can use or abuse.

Gods intends us to be sexual beings. That is not the same as saying God intends us all to be sexually active. We have noted that God sees human sexuality as good in itself. The creation narrative tells us that 'God created man in his own image ... male and female he created them' (Genesis1:27). Immediately 'God blessed them' (1:28) and commanded them to 'be fruitful and increase in number'. The creation of our sexuality and gender differences lies right at the heart of the Bible's creation account. Later in the Old Testament we find writings, like the Song of Songs, that celebrate human *eros* and use language with clearly erotic overtones. The New Testament accepts that we are sexual beings with powerful appetites. Its writers recognise the evil that a wrong use of these drives can produce. Clear guidelines are set down (see below).

The world's view of sex is not the one that God takes. Look around. The world debases the beauty of our sexuality. In its opposition to our Father God and to the Lord Jesus Christ the world uses sex for selfish gratification. It pressures you to be sexually active regardless of your marital status, and even regardless of age. Children as young as eleven or twelve are caught up in this. Older men corrupt younger girls. In some countries, like the United Kingdom, the medical profession uses codes of professional ethics that keep a parent right outside such a scenario, making medical confidentiality toward the child-patient a false excuse for inaction or exposing the child to serious physical or emotional risk.

That is how the world operates. It will tell you, by means of a thousand subtle hints and signals, that if you are not sexually experienced you cannot possibly be a complete person. Of course, this is arrant nonsense. The single, celibate life has been demonstrated over and over to be a full and authentic one, not least when it is lived for the sake of a sacred vocation. Look at Jesus, the most complete human being ever to walk on the planet. He was celibate, and perfect. He was sexually inactive, yet complete. He knows what it means to be male, to have been 'tempted in every way, just as we are' (Hebrews 4:15). So sexual temptation was faced and conquered by Jesus in the setting of a celibate life. We know He was 'without sin' (4:15). Here then is a picture of someone who was holy, celibate and normal.

Sexual love, *eros* love, love between a man and a woman, is a good thing if used according to God's laws. If we are not married we are meant to be celibate. Celibate means not engaging in any genital sexual activity. If we are Christian and single, others are entitled to assume we are therefore celibate. If we are not, we add deception to the sexual sin.

If we are married, we are meant to be sexually faithful (and faithful in all other ways) to our spouse. My wife is in an exclusive relationship with me, and I with her. This means there are bonds between us others cannot share. We have entered into sacred marriage covenants to which others cannot be a party. There are behaviours (covenant activities) that others cannot share. Sexual conduct is one of these. The Lord Jesus Christ teaches us that fidelity in a sexually exclusive relationship has to be taken very seriously indeed or the consequences can be disastrous. See Matthew 5:28 on this theme. Love between a man and a woman can be betrayed by a lustful glance, conduct that involves no touching. We must therefore make a further covenant, this time between oneself and one's eyes.

Sometimes sincere believers will ask where these standards of sexual behaviour can be found stated in the Bible. Knockdown proof texts are not the way to go. A little more thought is required. Search for a golden thread traceable through Scripture. Start in Genesis 2 where verse 24 is the first description in the Bible of marriage. This is part of the creation narrative and shows a man and a woman *publicly* leaving their parents to be *publicly* united by a *publicly* recognised ceremony. We know that all this was laced with a 'public' factor because Israelite weddings were as public as can be, with processions from one house to another, celebrations lasting days on end, and wedding feasts to which the entire community would be invited.

So the 'publicity factor' in the beginning of a sexual union is built into the Scriptures in passages where we are shown the mind of God for the ordering of human society. Marriage is God's invention, not man's. That may explain why there never has been a culture or a society in the entire history of the human race that did not use some form of marriage rites (whether religious or secular) to mark the onset of a sexual union.

Everyone in the community had a right to know (or at least the right to have access to the means of knowing) that a new relationship was about to begin, one that could result in new members of that community coming into it by birth. It is basic sociology. It was in the interests of the whole community. It still is. God knows best. (See also Chapter 6.)

We find further affirming of marriage in John 2 where Jesus accepts a wedding invitation. He could have declined it, thinking it a waste of time or money. However, He did not. He attended, thus affirming the bride and groom in their decision to marry before living together. Moreover, He used the setting of a wedding in which first to reveal His divine identity through miraculous action.

Later, in John 4, we find the Lord conversing with a woman beside a well. Verse 18 records His insight that she was living with a man without being married to him. This was definitely not said by way of congratulation!

The Corinthian letters can help here too. 1 Corinthians 6:12-20 teaches that our bodies are indwelt by the Spirit of God when we are born again in Christ. This is not a poetic metaphor. It is to be taken literally. So what we do with our bodies draws Christ himself into the action. The illustration used by Paul is that of sexual intercourse outside marriage. His next chapter (see 7:9, 36) has wise counsel for the unmarried person encountering strong sexual temptations. The Bible's advice is to marry. The advice is not to find a woman to sleep with. It is to marry. Moreover, the marriage is to be to a believer (2 Corinthians 6:14). This may have application far beyond marriage, for there are more ways than one to be 'yoked together with unbelievers'. The world of business is but one obvious example.

In Ephesians 5:21-33 Paul writes eloquently about marriage. He uses the married relationship to draw out teaching about the relationship between Christ and his 'bride', the church. Paul does not use the example of a couple having sex outside marriage. Rather, he chooses marriage to illustrate Christ's commitment – as public and open, on the Cross, as any commitment ever could be – to the church. Conversely, he uses Christ's commitment to us to teach us about the true nature of marriage.

All this reveals marriage as holding a high value in the eyes of God. Marriage ought therefore to be similarly placed in our human estimation. This is not achieved by discarding or bypassing it.

Psalm 51 reveals the consequences of sexual sin. Written after its author, David, had engaged in sexual wrongdoing, it shows that such actions carry with them the risk that the Holy Spirit will leave us. 'Do not cast me from your presence or take your Holy Spirit from me,' cried David (51:11). The risks are huge. They have eternal dimensions. They are associated with all sin, but here especially with sexual sin. We need to remember that the risks are not only carried by the sinners, but are also run by those who have teaching or leadership roles in the Body of Christ and yet do not uphold and declare courageously, in a spirit of *agape* love, these divinely appointed laws.

The love the Greeks called *eros* is one of God's most precious gifts to mankind. He bestowed it intentionally. He knew what he was doing. He saw it as good. He intends us to use and enjoy it. He has set down the pattern for this. The holy life does not involve a turning away from our sexuality. The celibate, single and sanctified person is still a sexual creature, even though his or her sexuality is not meant to be expressed in a physical relationship. Sexuality is deeper and wider than genital activity. The married, sanctified person will be as sexually pure within the married state as was our Lord in his singleness, and as committed to their spouse as was the Lord to our salvation at Calvary. All this comes about when *eros* love seeks the transforming influence of *agape* love. To be fully what God intended, both *philia* and *eros* must submit to heaven-love, to what the Greeks called *agape*.

The love that comes from heaven – agape

It was John Gowans who penned the line: 'From your love my love is learning.' The full verse goes like this:

Burning, burning, gently burning,
Gently burning Fire within,

From your love my love is learning,
Now I feel your work begin.

The third line of this verse is precisely about love that comes from heaven (*agape*) acting upon human loves (*philia* and *eros*) so that all our love, whether directed to a spouse, family, friend, neighbour or fellow believer is permeated with the love of God shown in Christ. This is a very real and practical thing that happens to Christians. It is a consequence of the blessing of a clean heart, which Commissioner Samuel Brengle characterised as a baptism of love. It is part of that divinely initiated process of character transformation that is central to living a holy life.

Heaven-love goes on loving even when not returned. It is self-sufficient, unlike *philia* or *eros*. It is the love that God has for us. It is the love that can love an enemy or pray for a persecutor (Matthew 5:43, 44). It is seen in Jesus. It is Cross-shaped. For Jesus, exercising heaven-love was agony. It was painful, costly, lonely, thorn-ridden. It was dark, nail-pierced, and blood red. It was worth it, for it spells our salvation and takes us to heaven.

Heaven-love is the very essence of God's holy nature. God *is* love (1 John 4:16). He will not act contrary to this. He cannot harm us when we live in His will. He offers us the marvellous possibility of being in union with Jesus, like a vine to its branches (John 15). From heaven comes eternal, unfathomed, unquenchable love. It flows in never ceasing abundance through Jesus, our Saviour, to flood and re-flood our hearts, to change us into His likeness, and to show the world that we are His.

Heaven-love is a fruit of the Holy Spirit. It grows in us when we come to Christ. It is the fruit above all other fruits, binding the rest together. Its presence in us is the one infallible evidence that we are Spirit-filled. It is also a gift of the Holy Spirit above all other gifts (1 Corinthians 13). It is the gift by which all others are tested. Its absence renders other gifts of the Spirit meaningless.

Heaven-love is Jesus. It defies definition. It cannot be described. It must be felt, received, yielded to. It is not for embracing, for it embraces. It is not for measuring, for by it all are measured. It is not for possessing, for through it we are possessed. Heaven-love (1 Corinthians 13) is kind and patient, never envies, never boasts, knows no undue pride, is ever courteous, seeks nothing for itself, is not easily angered, bears no grudge, knows evil when it sees it, and delights in righteousness. Heaven-love *is* Jesus. When everything else has passed, heaven-love lives on. Sanctity lives on. Holiness lives on. Those baptised by heaven-love live on. We shall be a holy people, seeing face to face and at last understanding fully in the presence of a holy God.

CHAPTER 4

BELIEVE, THEN ACT

HOLINESS AND ETHICS

PROFESSOR John Barton of Oxford University in his *Ethics and the Old Testament* (London, SCM Press Ltd, 1998) writes of moral conduct springing up out of gratitude to God, inspired by God's holiness and the divine love for us. The great Dietrich Bonhoeffer's *Ethics* (London, Collins Fontana, 1970) also sees a clear causal connection between ethical conduct on our part and the holiness of God.

Yet you have to read an awful lot of the Old Testament before you come across any absolutely clear understanding of the impact a belief in the holiness of God could or should have upon individual personal conduct. Centuries passed before 'the Lord is holy' was allowed to become a theological ground for personal ethics or individual righteousness. Today we do not even pause to question this link. However, it was not always so. In the earliest days of the events found in the Old Testament, 'holy' meant simply 'separate' or 'other'. It carried no sense of 'morally pure' or 'good'.

Only the Lord was holy. In absolute contrast, his creatures were regarded as exactly the opposite. So any idea of reflected holiness in a human being was at first pretty far fetched. Then certain places came to be associated with the presence of the Lord, and these also came to be seen as holy. It was God's presence that made them so. Then special seasons or days were devoted to the Lord, and holy status was accorded these too. Next, if things like candlesticks, cups or containers were used in holy places at holy times it was logical also to call them holy.

So what about holy people? Yes, in the end Israelite thinking came to encompass this revolutionary idea. Religious law codes were devised to lead the community into righteousness and eventually, in passages like Jeremiah 31: 31-34, we discover that the law of righteousness, God's 'new covenant with the house of Israel', will be 'within them' and God 'will write it upon their hearts'. At last a direct theological connection was being made between a belief in the holiness of God and the impact that belief could and should have on the personal behaviour of the believer. Religious belief leading to holy action had been invented! It had taken centuries, but it was worth it!

So steeped are we in the writings of the New Testament, and especially of Paul who found it impossible to do theology in purely abstract terms, that this linkage between faith and ethics is taken almost for granted. This short essay revisits that linkage in the hope of teasing out something more about how it all works in practice for Salvationists. I think we are down to earth folk, like Paul. When we preach, whatever the theological theme, we usually end up applying it to personal conduct. In other words, we intuit the need to believe first, and then act.

Does it not seem odd then that, in the Army, when we mention 'ethics' we mostly mean our various positional statements on social ethical issues? We do not often use the word to mean the things you and I do each day by way of personal conduct. Now here is a strange thing because ethics is first and foremost about personal, individual behaviour. I have already suggested that we understand well the faith basis for godly standards in this area. Nearly every Army worship service will have content that is premised on this understanding, and especially when our doctrine of sanctification or holiness is being expounded. I say again, however, that we do not often refer to personal behaviour as 'ethics'. It is 'your life' or 'lifestyle' or 'your need' (to be more loving, etc.). On the other hand, when we do use the word 'ethics' it is likely we will be referring to a public issue of some sort or perhaps to a professional ethical code. In this area we have not accomplished all that much explicit theology, and this contrasts strongly with our approach to personal ethics. Few of our positional statements contain theological rationale. They are too short for that. Furthermore, it is nearly twenty years since we published a serious book on social ethics. That was in 1985 and before that we had published only one or two in the whole of our history.

Salvationists are thus a people who do not often refer to personal conduct as 'ethics' but who nevertheless ground their behavioural standards theologically. Conversely, they seem to use 'ethics' narrowly to mean social ethics without offering much by way of an explicit theological basis issue by issue. Ideally we would recognise both personal behaviour and social issues as 'ethical', and we would take the time and trouble to ground it all explicitly in religious and doctrinal belief.

Our literature abounds with material on personal holiness. It is true that we need more of this of a modern kind, but we have enough to help us through until new prophets of holiness arise among us. What we have not done, it seems to me, is to explore adequately the basis that our holiness doctrine provides for social action (in contradistinction to social service) and for striking various stances on social ethical issues. *Why* do we say what we say about homosexuality? *Why* do we say what we say about race relations? *Why* do we say what we say about abortion? I believe the real answers to these questions lie buried in our holiness teaching. It is an exploration, perhaps an excavation, waiting – nay, crying out – to be undertaken.

At this point I need to refer to the November 2002 issue of *Word and Deed* (Alexandria, The Salvation Army, Vol. 5, No. 1) in which Major John G. Merritt offers a helpful article touching on this matter. He writes of the need for 'doctrinal fidelity *and* ethical integrity' (italics mine). You cannot have the second without the first. This cannot be said often, or loudly, enough. I hope we in the Army can go further over time and embark upon an explicit exploration of the relationship between our Tenth Doctrine and each of the ethical social issues on which we have taken up a formal, publicly stated position. So the questions would shape up something like this (these are just a few examples and we could frame similar questions arising out of the other ten Articles of Faith):

- If we accept the Tenth Doctrine, how will that shape our position on abortion or on euthanasia? How will that determine not only what we say, but how we say it and when and to whom?
- If we are preaching and teaching sanctification, what will that mean for working out a position on poverty, or war, or terrorism, or family violence?
- If we believe it is the privilege of all believers to be wholly sanctified, what are the direct or indirect consequences for addressing the lawmaking programmes in our federal and state legislatures?

Let us ponder this a little longer. Everybody's favourite definition of holiness is the one that says 'Holiness is Christ in you' or 'Holiness is Christlikeness'. Now putting it this way certainly helps to keep us from too arid a presentation of the doctrine and retains an essential focus on Jesus and His holy example as 'truly and properly man' (see Doctrine 4). From this starting point it is natural and right to see obedience to the commands of Christ as the pivotal basis for holiness. Dietrich Bonhoeffer, to whom I referred at the beginning of this essay, tells us that formation or conformation to the likeness of Christ is at the heart of an ethical life. Christian ethics, for Bonhoeffer, is transformative conformation to Jesus Christ. In Jesus we can see all we need to see of God. So Bonhoeffer urges us not to ask 'How can I be good?' or 'How can I do good?' but instead ask, 'What is the will of God?' The answer is that the will of God is realised in Christ. In this way all questions about good, all moral questions, become a question of to what extent we are willing to participate in the divine reality which is revealed in Christ.

With this in mind, it is natural to come to the words of Christ's New Commandment in John 13:34. We are to love as Jesus has loved us. It is the love God has for us. It is given unconditionally, needs nothing in return in order to survive, and is available to ordinary believers for the asking (John 14:12-14). If all this is true, what then are the implications for taking up any Army ethical position? What does it mean lovingly (*agape*istically), and in accordance with the New Commandment of Christ, to pronounce on divorce, or on pre-marital sex and cohabiting, or on the use of alcohol, and so on?

In such an exercise, who is it that we are meant to be loving in obedience to John 13:34? Is it the community in which we live and witness, members of minorities, the marginalised and poor, the rich and powerful who might be oppressing them, our lawmakers, our political leaders, the press and broadcasting media who will want to examine what we say if we put our Salvationist heads above the secular parapet? How can you love an institution like a legislature? Does our Tenth Doctrine help? I believe it does. Somewhere within the Scriptural truths that the Doctrine seeks to encapsulate are the answers to these questions and many others like them. God grant us the mind and the energy to think it all through.

Meanwhile, like many of you, I must press on intuitively as each occasion gives rise to the next public ethical issue. As I write, here in New Zealand (a land that is beautiful beyond description yet fallen like Eden after the apple) the Army has been seeking a loving (*agapeistic*) mind on some recent high profile public issues. I mention these by way of practical illustration of the ways in which we have been seeking, under God, to let our belief shape our ethics. We have tried to believe, and then act.

1. The military action in Iraq in 2003 (see Chapter 5) gave rise to three public statements by the New Zealand church leaders. The Army played its part in wording these and signed them all. So, in addition to calling the Salvationists of New Zealand, Fiji and Tonga to prayer, we have sought – while shunning all political naivety – to obey the Lord's command in a spirit of a) holiness, and b) tough love toward the following: Saddam Hussein, the people of Iraq, the United States of America and her allies, the United Nations, the American and British diplomatic staff in Wellington, and the New Zealand Prime Minister and her government. With all this has come also the unexpected need to obey the New Commandment toward a few fundamentalist, evangelical church leaders (they are part of John 13:34's 'one another') who viewed the attack on Iraq as preordained by God and therefore felt unable to sign the various statements by the national church leaders.

2. We have faced legal reforms in the law on prostitution and have tried to speak with a Christian voice. The legal process has been long and drawn out. This has led to a gradual change of attitude among some Salvationists. What was said to Parliament two years ago no longer seemed all that tenable. So suddenly we, the people of the Tenth Doctrine, were required to be *agapeistic* toward the Salvationists who drew up the first official Army response to the Bill, toward the politicians using our name to bolster their own stance, toward the sex workers who were to be affected by the Bill (among some of whom we have ministry) and, finally, toward their clients whose conduct would not be changed one bit by legislation. We have had to think quickly. We were sought out for

our views. Each word had to be weighed in the light of our Tenth Doctrine. With no time to reflect in leisurely style, we relied on God the Holy Spirit to keep us alert and intelligent for Christ and for the people.

3. During all this, a Bill was introduced into Parliament to legalise euthanasia. It was called (strangely) the Death with Dignity Bill. Again, the Army – a holiness people – needed to be heard. We were being called upon to take a position in clear opposition to the Bill, and yet to be loving toward the lawmaker who sponsored the measure (his wife had died a slow and tragic death), the families of others who had suffered terminal illnesses, those presently diagnosed as terminally ill, the medical profession, and the members of Parliament who would have to vote on the Bill. We decided to send a personalised letter to all members of Parliament from the leadership of the territory. Happily, the Bill was defeated on its first reading in the national legislature.

We turn instinctively to the Scriptures whenever such issues confront us. There we are impacted again by the eternal word of God. Divinely revealed truths shape our minds and hearts and help us think through issues of war, issues of life and death, issues of sexual mores. Often Scripture will offer no specific word on a particular issue. That is when we need to soak ourselves afresh in the tenets of holiness, seeking out – and pleading in prayer for – the mind of Christ.

CHAPTER 5

'ANGELS IN THE RAFTERS'

HOLINESS AND TERRORISM

Personal memories

BORN in Belfast, Northern Ireland, I was always aware of terrorism as a tool used by the ruthless to achieve their goals. However, it was not until The Salvation Army sent my wife, Helen, and me to Rhodesia (now Zimbabwe) in 1975 that I came face to face with the reality of it. In the late 1970's Rhodesia was in the grip of a guerilla / terrorist struggle to oust the exclusively white government of Prime Minister Ian Smith.

Those of us living and working in rural settings faced the daily possibility of terrorist action. It was far from easy. Having a small toddler son (Matthew) and a baby daughter (Jenny) added to the tensions. Frequently we asked ourselves what right we had to expose them to risk. The terrorist attack on the Army's Usher Institute, a boarding school for girls, in mid-1978 brought it all to a head (see Henry Gariepy, *Mobilised for God – The History of The Salvation Army, Volume 8, 1977-1994*, Grand Rapids, Eerdmans, 2000, pp. 16-19). It fell to me to be the first to reach the school, after staff had been killed and wounded, to effect the evacuation of the students. The memory of identifying the bodies of two young women colleagues will never leave me.

The risks faced some years later in Lahore, Pakistan were perhaps less direct, but equally real. White faces were always a possible target for extremists in this Islamic Republic. Christians in general, both expatriate and indigenous, were vulnerable. For nearly five years we lived and worked each day guarded by armed security personnel. World events could heighten the dangers at very short notice.

September 11, 2001

It was in our quarters in Lahore that I found myself unable to leave the TV screen on September 11, 2001, as hijacked planes were flown into the twin towers of the World Trade Centre in New York and into the Pentagon building in Washington. Fiendishness! Naked evil! Satanic disregard for humanity! No words could capture what we were seeing.

Bemused CNN and BBC reporters tried in vain to piece it all together.

Today the impressions tumble through my mind: desolated loved ones; tears, unending tears; suffering Americans, dignified but hurting; the death toll mounting; dead from many nations; pain, searing pain of heart and mind; eloquent tributes to the dead and the rescue teams; Salvationism at its very best, round the clock at Ground Zero; universal disgust at what had been done; sympathy welling up in huge waves for all affected; renewed human solidarity in the face of evil.

All we could do was reel with the horrible shock. Pakistani Salvationists turned instinctively to prayer for the victims and for America as a nation. We were soon to be in the firing line too when the USA response was characterised as a 'crusade', a term resurrecting Moslem memories of the ancient Christian Crusades against Islam. The Moslem world braced itself for what was perceived as a new Christian retaliatory attack upon its values and religion. Christians in Pakistan, especially westerners, prepared themselves for reprisals. These came.

Then, suddenly, the Cruise missiles. Wakened one night in October 2001 by a buzzing mosquito, we rose and made tea. The BBC was reporting the first assault on our near neighbours in Afghanistan. Most foreigners had left Pakistan by then. The Salvation Army missionaries were among the few to remain throughout. It was not pleasant, but we tried to see things in proportion. We could not leave our Pakistani colleagues. The risk of reprisals was as much theirs as ours.

Is anywhere safe?

Modern terrorism can leave us feeling that nowhere is safe. Can there have been a time when so many 'travel advisory' warnings have gone out from governments world-wide? Even 'essential' travel is being curtailed. Place names like Jakarta, Bali, Oklahoma City, Kashmir, East Timor, Jerusalem, Chechnya, Omagh, Casablanca, Yemen, or Baghdad create deep-seated, chilling ripples of apprehension. R.T. Kendall, an American pastor, has expressed many of our feelings in his threefold summation: nowhere seems safe any more; no one is secure any more;

nothing is shocking any more – *The Day the World Changed* (London, Hodder and Stoughton, 2001).

The US Department of Homeland Security, created in the aftermath of September 11, has inherited the workforces, programmes and infrastructure of the Coast Guard, the Customs Service, the Immigration and Naturalisation Service, and the Transportation Security Administration. The security task is huge. Each year in America 730 million people travel on commercial aircraft and there are 700 million pieces of baggage to be screened for explosives. Add to this the 11.2 million trucks, the 2.2 million rail cars, and the 7,500 'foreign flag' ships that enter the States annually and the size of the challenge to keep people safe in that one country alone becomes apparent.

The Rt. Rev. Dr. Michael Nazir-Ali is a Pakistani by birth and a Church of England bishop serving in England. In *Understanding my Moslem Neighbour* (London, SPCK, 2002) he warns that terrorism is here to stay. He foresees matters getting much worse if we fail to realise that conflicts in places like Israel, Palestine, Kashmir, Chechnya, Bosnia and Kosovo are not only the locations of terrorism but the causes as well. He argues for a resolution to the Middle East tensions, without which terrorism will flourish and expand. For those in the Moslem world, the policies of the west toward Palestine and the Arab states generally are seen as intolerably one sided. Until this changes, Bishop Nazir-Ali sees no end to terrorism. That same terrorism will, moreover, manifest itself all over the world and not only in Middle East locations. For Moslem non-moderates (a minority of Moslems but whose numbers run into tens of millions) it is a global struggle against a 'Christian' west.

Types of terrorism

It is tempting to speak of 'terrorism' as though it were a single, monolithic phenomenon. It is not. It comes in many different forms. A useful summary of the major terrorist groups around the world can be found in the US State Department's annual publication, *Patterns of Global Terrorism*, available on the Internet at www.state.gov. See also Executive

Order 13224 at the same site. Readers wishing to delve more deeply are referred to Barrie Paskins and Michael Dockrill, *The Ethics of War* (London, Duckworth, 1979), pp. 58-101.

We hear of economic terrorism, psychological terrorism, environmental terrorism, nuclear terrorism, and many other manifestations that may or may not have close connections to politics or international relations. Then there is state terrorism, sponsored by governments. Sometimes terrorism is linked to organised crime syndicates. The motives of terrorists are as varied as their many causes. Basically, however, all terrorism is aimed at inducing fear. This is attempted, not in a spontaneous or random way, but by premeditated and planned actions. The methods are specific and intentional. The intent is to arouse deep, instinctive fear in persons other than the direct victims, so as to make the wider audience (a government or part of the population) change its policies or attitudes.

It helps if we distinguish between terrorist groups with defined and stated political goals, and those whose motives seem less defined, sometimes known as apocalyptic terrorists aiming to control or destroy the world. The first type of terrorism can be assuaged by political change. These are the activists who are seen as terrorists by some but as freedom fighters by others. It was such as these that struck the Usher Institute in 1978 (see above). Examples today are found in Chechnya, Northern Ireland, Afghanistan, and Palestine. The destruction they leave in their wake is appalling. In ten years 100,000 civilians have died in Chechnya and 200,000 displaced. In Afghanistan the legacy of the Taliban (who sheltered the Al-Qaeda network) has yet to be revealed in all its brutality. In Northern Ireland countless innocent citizens have been shot or bombed to death over political arguments that have been a running sore for generations.

Religiously motivated terrorism

Apocalyptic terrorists, on the other hand, are not open to being deflected by political change or appeasement. These tend to be religiously motivated and are seen as fanatical in their cause.

About 25% of known terrorist groups are driven by religious motives. Between 1970 and 1995 there were no fewer than 64,000 recorded terrorist incidents and over half of these were attributable to religious terrorism. When Prime Minister Yitzhak Rabin of Israel was killed in 1995, his assassin said, 'I acted alone and on orders from God.' It was followers of the Japanese Aum Shinrikyo sect who released nerve gas into the Tokyo subway. Extremist Moslems say that martyrdom is the ultimate victory. The decades long violence in Northern Ireland is in the name of Christianity. No religion is exempt from being abused in such ways ('zealot', 'assassin' and 'thug' are terms derived from Judaism, Islam and Hinduism respectively). Not only terrorism, but whole wars are fought in the name of religion, and we sometimes hear government reactions to terrorism justified in similarly religious terms.

Contemporary responses to terrorism

Responses to terrorism have ranged through the years from appeasement to all out pre-emptive military strikes, characterised as 'war'.

Appeasement has been shown to encourage further acts of terror. The temptation to yield to the demands of the terrorist is, however, a powerful one. In the UK Prime Minister Tony Blair agreed to open the prison gates in Northern Ireland and let convicted terrorists, killers and bombers walk free, in the hope of buying an end to the violence carried out for decades by the Irish Republican Army (IRA) and other paramilitary groups. Ironically, the home-grown terrorists were being overtly appeased even as the UK government talked and acted tough on terrorism beyond its own borders, not least on the evils of terror carried out in the USA. In August 2003, as this essay was being written, the IRA was demanding next that the British government should delete for ever all criminal records of the 15,000 IRA members convicted of terror offences, including murder. They claimed these acts were acts of war against an occupying British force in Northern Ireland.

Germany, France and Italy have been accused of adopting policies of appeasement through the years, one famous example being when the Israeli athletes were murdered at the 1972 Olympic Games in Munich. Three terrorists were captured but never brought to trial. They were later released in exchange for hijacked Germans on board a Lufthansa flight.

At the other end of the spectrum from appeasement is the response of all-out military attack. In the aftermath of September 11, 2001 and in the light of (subsequently doubted) claims about weapons of mass destruction, the UK and USA governments attacked both Afghanistan and Iraq, the latter with help from Australia. These attacks were justified politically and militarily by reference to the 'doctrine' of the pre-emptive strike. Let us take time to reflect in a non-partisan manner and objectively on this basis for going to war against another nation in response to individual criminal acts of terror.

We know that terrorism is not going to go away. It is part of modern life. It is not a new phenomenon. What is strikingly new is the act of going (literally) to war as a response. This has come to replace or augment a response based on the process of law and order using the criminal justice systems of the world. At first many thought that talk of a 'war on terror' was rhetoric only, like speaking of a 'war on crime' or a 'war on drugs' or a 'war on litter'. It was taken as a (not unreasonable) trumpet call to point up the seriousness of it all. Very soon, however, it became clear that those using this language were deadly serious about war. They meant literally that they would take their nations to war, just as much as during the two World Wars or as in Vietnam. Yet there was no defined enemy nation or coalition of nations. There were no battle lines. It was to be a new type of war for the 21st century.

Whatever our political views, we need to be aware that this development seeks to redefine war. It brings an entirely new dynamic into international relations. Some secular and some Christian commentators have welcomed it. Others are more cautious for it is not yet clear that the pre-emptive strike 'doctrine' is in the best long-term interests of the human race or of the family of nations.

Politically impartial reflection allows us to note that no such 'doctrine' is known to or recognised by international law. It has been birthed in political circles. Ingrid De Lupis, in her *The Law of War* (Cambridge, Cambridge University Press, 1987), a book of over 400 pages which contributes to the 'Monographs in International Studies' series for the London School of Economics and Political Science, dismisses the concept in seven lines. The magisterial work by Paskins and Dockrill (see above) makes no mention of it whatsoever.

Does the world need to stop and look very carefully before allowing this theory to take hold and determine lethal actions? Is it not the case that if the UK can use the 'doctrine', then so too can Iran or Russia? If the USA can use it, cannot Pakistan, Palestine or North Korea invoke it too? If Australia adopts it, then what is to stop Indonesia or China doing so as well? It will not for long be the prerogative of one state or a small group of western states only. Any state, including those seen as terrorist states, will claim that a disliked or feared neighbour – or a feared super power far away – should be pre-emptively attacked in case of what they might one day do.

It yet remains to be seen whether or not international law will embrace and bless a claimed right to go in and destroy a regime, at whatever cost and without any clear plan for that nation's future, not because of what has been done to you, but because of what you cannot prove might one day be done to you. Many (though not all) Christian commentators believe that this 'doctrine' will increase, rather than diminish, the violence in the world. Worthy of note is the 'Urgent Call' issued on May 6, 2003 by those who attended an interfaith summit in Chicago just as the first phase of the war in Iraq was ending. Co-convened by the USA National Council of Churches, the 'Call' included this plea: 'We say to the present leadership of the United States to draw back from the use and threat of first strike war.' Representing The Salvation Army among the signatories was the Territorial Commander for the USA Central Territory.

Christians have held to the tried and tested principles of the 'just war' as prudent parameters for initiating (and continuing) military action amounting to war. Just war principles have at their heart three concepts: discrimination, proportion and success – see my *Strong Doctrine, Strong*

Mercy (London, The Salvation Army, 1985), Chapter 8. Let us see what emerges when these principles are applied objectively to war as a response to criminal actions involving terror, in contrast to responding through the international law enforcement and criminal justice system options.

Discrimination, proportion and success

For countless generations now the church has said that for wartime military action to be morally justified it must differentiate between combatants and non-combatants. It must seek actively to target only other military personnel or installations. This is the principle of discrimination. Military action that is reckless of whether or not innocent civilians are killed is deemed immoral according to 'just war' thinking, and illegal under international law. The high numbers of innocent civilians killed or wounded in Afghanistan and Iraq tell a story that cannot be ignored, one that may well come to be seen by history as being as powerful and poignant as the innocent suffering in the west which preceded the invasion of those states.

The principle of proportion calls for military action to be kept to the lowest possible level. I confess to puzzling over the massive military assault on Afghanistan, one of the feeblest, poorest nations on earth. As we followed events from Lahore in neighbouring Pakistan, we wondered why thousands more had to die. Neither my wife nor I have ever held pacifist convictions. Moreover, we were in anguish about the terror perpetrated on America, a land in which we had lived so very happily and where we had and have many friends. We knew the wrongdoers had to be most vigorously pursued and brought to justice, and we were in fact praying for that to happen. However, try as we might, we could not make ethical or theological sense of *war* being launched. It seemed the age of the blunderbuss had returned to replace the scalpel. Innocent people were being further sacrificed, when a response of measured, lethal precision remained a viable option. 'Keep it in proportion,' the non-pacifist theologians have said to the politicians for centuries. The violence should be of a kind and at a level that will accomplish your aim, and no more.

The theologians have also urged state leaders to calculate the chances of success before going to war. This is in order to ensure that the outcome of war does not produce a scenario worse than that the war seeks to remedy. Readers will make up their own minds as to whether the invasion of Afghanistan, if we take that as a working example, has been a 'success'.

On the positive side, the repressive Taliban have been scattered. Al Qaeda camps have been destroyed. Women and girls can once more be educated outside the home and pursue working careers. Music can be heard in the streets of Kabul. Attempts are in hand to form a national police force and army, things never previously accomplished in feudal Afghanistan.

On the negative side, the new Vice-President (Haji Abdul Qadir) has been assassinated. Innocent civilians have been killed in large numbers by occupying forces. Local warlords, armed and enriched by western cash paid over to induce them to fight against the Taliban, are still killing others. The new interim government announces its intention to be less barbaric than the Taliban – it will not behead or amputate criminals in public in the football stadium, but will now do it in private. The poppy growers are free again to cultivate their deadly plants. Local warlords feud and murder. The rule of law, enforced by NATO troops, does not extend beyond Kabul. The fate of the notorious Osama bin Laden is still not known. Despairing civilians have limped over the border into Pakistan where it fell to my Salvation Army staff of the Pakistan Territory, with solid help from the Army internationally (including from the UK and USA), to add to the feeding programmes in Peshawar for these victims. Success can be an elusive goal.

The sanctified mind

So far in this essay we have looked informationally at factual and background aspects of terrorism. Let us move now to a consideration of forming a spiritual outlook. What might 'the sanctified mind' make of it all?

1. Trusting

The sanctified mind, in the face of terrorism, and even in the midst of dreadful suffering all around, will go on trusting in God. Job said, 'Though He slay me, yet will I trust Him' (13:15, AV). This means still believing in, and acting upon, the goodness of God. It also means never giving up one's hold on God's ultimate sovereignty, even if present circumstances or events offer little evidence of this. Bible passages such as Psalm 37, Isaiah 40, and Revelation 21 can inspire in us a perspective, a calmness of heart and spirit, that is of God even when the evil seems invincible.

2. Understanding

The sanctified mind will make the effort involved to understand what is going on. It will not settle for newspaper headline slogans or the shrill voices of political leaders or media commentators. It will look deeper than that. The sanctified mind will be an informed mind, furnished with relevant facts, and unwilling to be swayed by the loudest voices. A mind modelled on the mind of Christ will not accept blindly the opinions of the politicians or the media commentators. It will instead wrestle with the moral issues at stake and be ready to say, if need be, that what is morally wrong can never be politically right.

3. Praying

The sanctified mind will go to prayer. A formal statement issued by The Salvation Army in the USA on the war in Iraq (*War Cry*, April 26, 2003) and entitled 'Hope, Strength, Love' signally declined to endorse the political stance of the American government over Iraq (see the Appendix to this Chapter). Instead it placed strong emphasis on the call to prayer – prayer for divine intervention in the hearts of human leaders, and for speedy, peaceful solutions to be found.

The sanctified mind will pray knowing that there is a way through that does not always lie in taking up the weapons of the big battalions. David could not even lift the armour he was offered when going to face Goliath, yet Goliath ended up face down in the sand as the result of a measured, lethally precise response. Jesus stilled the storm with only a word, and explicitly rejected the 'legions' option when being arrested.

Pastor R.T. Kendall has called for Christians to engage not only in praying, but to undertake 'gracious praying'. This is a task for the sanctified mind. When most are crying out for vengeance and retaliation, gracious praying prays for the terrorists – for their capture, yes, but also for their souls' salvation and for their forgiveness (see 10 below). Jesus has commanded us to love our enemies unconditionally (Luke 6: 27-31) and this is something that takes supernatural power. The sanctified mind knows this and seeks it in prayer.

4. Listening

The sanctified mind is alert to the myriad voices that crowd in when trouble and terror strike. It does not filter out the screams of the victims. It hears and weeps with them and their loved ones. Neither does it filter out the dubious rationalisations and fanatical assertions from the perpetrators, because hearing these is part of seeking understanding. All this takes divine grace, for our human instincts run counter to it.

Then there are the diverse Christian voices. Some will say the terrorists are demons, others that they have a case that needs to be heard even though their methods are evil. Some voices will be raised attempting to speak for the Body of Christ as a whole or some part of the Body. President George Bush's own church, the United Methodist Church, came out against the war on Iraq. A group of over forty bishops and pastors of Protestant and Orthodox churches asked the President to meet with them, on behalf of the 38 denominations that form the National Council of Churches in America. Leaders of the Roman Catholic, Episcopal, Presbyterian and Methodist churches expressed strong opposition to the war. Gathered at 10 Downing Street, London, American mainline church leaders told Prime Minister Tony Blair that never before had the churches of America been so united in opposing government policy on a war issue (similar stances were taken by the principal denominations in the United Kingdom). The sanctified mind will pray for religious leaders making public statements, and for the political leaders and others to whom their words are sent. (See further the Appendix to Chapter 5.)

5. Recognising evil

The sanctified mind will never cease to recognise the stark reality of evil. There will be no making of excuses for sinful actions. Even while praying for one's enemy, his evil ways and motives will not be overlooked. The sanctified mind is down-to-earth about what evil can accomplish, and thus invokes all the power of Heaven (Ephesians 6:10-18) to overcome it according to God's purposes and timing.

6. Not demonising

Even so, the sanctified mind will not join in the general clamour to demonise the terrorists. Though their ways be evil, their motives wrong, and their actions deadly, they are still human beings. In demonising them we diminish ourselves and sink to their level as they demonise their targets and the governments they despise. The tendency to demonise our enemies is our chief obstacle in understanding them. Failure to understand them diminishes the chances of overcoming them.

7. Respecting other faiths

The sanctified mind will remain open to the reality that not all who share the religion of the terrorist approve of his actions. Not all Moslems are terrorists, and neither are all Christians. Islam is in fact a religion that is primarily about unity – the unity of God and the unity of the community under God. The clear majority of Moslems regretted deeply and condemned openly what took place on September 11, 2001.

The sanctified mind, though knowing that Christ is uniquely and supremely the Saviour of mankind, will nevertheless be willing to see good in other faiths and in their adherents, even if not accepting their beliefs. The world today needs, perhaps as never before, education across faith boundaries so that interfaith understanding and dialogue can increase. Too often we see and hear evidence of 'blinkered' belief, as though we have nothing to learn from others. Islamophobia, the unreasonable fear of all Moslems, is spreading rapidly and is an ugly thing, unworthy of those who follow Jesus.

The sanctified mind, steeped in the things of Christ, will respect the faith of others and pray for mutual interfaith understanding and peace everywhere. At the same time it will remain rooted in the uniqueness of Christ and His saving work at Calvary, from which arises a passion for people of all faiths, or of none, to give their allegiance to Him.

8. No vengeance

The sanctified mind does not seek vengeance for itself or for others. Scripture teaches us that vengeance belongs to the Lord, not to us (Romans 12:19). Those living a holy life will be keenly alive to the evils of terrorism, but instead of crying out for vengeance or revenge, will seek simply an end to terrorism. This is a laudable goal. Vengeance is not.

9. Loving our neighbour

Even the deadliest, lowest, meanest acts of terrorism cannot abrogate the Scriptures or the teaching of Christ. In the modern world, love of neighbour takes on new meanings. The question, 'Who is my neighbour?' has to be answered now in new ways because the world is shrinking rapidly. We live more and more in a global village where almost everyone on the planet is sooner or later, in some sense, my neighbour. Thus the terrorist is my ill-intentioned neighbour, in need of being stopped. The terrorist's family, though far away, may also be my neighbour in the global village and I am simply not permitted to extend to his relatives my feelings about his actions. Still less am I free to tar all his fellow countrymen with the same terrorist brush.

In fact, love of neighbour goes still further than the mere absence of hatred. It requires us to be interested in the problems of the terrorist's homeland. Moral obligation in today's small world goes far beyond family, or tribe, or nation. We need to feel sometimes that total strangers are our neighbours, committing ourselves to people we know nothing about. Modern communications have brought this about. Pictures on our TV screens have widened our moral imagination and we see today an army of missionaries, aid workers (including Salvationists in post-war Iraq), reporters, human rights observers and so on leaving home for the sake of others. Michael Ignatieff has explored this brilliantly in his penetrating analysis of ethnic war, *The Warrior's Honour* (London, Vintage, 1999).

10. Forgiving

The sanctified mind knows that forgiveness and total realism about the evil of terrorism can co-exist. Forgiveness and punishment can also co-exist, as I have argued in *Strong Doctrine, Strong Mercy* (London, The Salvation Army, 1985), pp. 88-93. So a plea to come to the point of forgiving the terrorist does not thereby rule out the vigorous, intentional, determined pursuit of him, or his capture and eventual punishment. Further, forgiveness, while holding within it the seeds of eventually transforming the evildoer, is also about what we are willing or unwilling to do to ourselves. A refusal to forgive will embitter us. Bitterness can be a killer in its own right for it kills the spirit of the one who harbours it. It is a terrorist within.

USA Pastor R.T. Kendall, quoted earlier, called for 'total forgiveness' after September 11 (*The Day the World Changed*). He reminds us that when all around are crying out for retaliation, those seeking the sanctified mind are being presented with an unprecedented opportunity to show that rarest of things – total forgiveness. We are reminded, albeit somewhat uncomfortably, of the words of our crucified and risen Lord: 'Love your enemies, do good to those who hate you, bless those who curse you, pray for those who mistreat you … If you love those who love you, what credit is that to you?' (Luke 6: 27-32).

Here is a prayer I wrote, when looking back on the attack of September 11, one year after it took place:

Help me see it in proportion, Lord.
Somewhere, somehow, sometime, Lord, we need to speak forgiveness.
I need to do this, Lord, for those who hated me and mine and my fellow

Christians in Pakistan, breathing out murderous threats
like Saul of old.
Does forgiveness still work, Lord?
Give me a sense of proportion, Lord.
I am on my knees before you:
for a world paralysed by fear;
for Americans, suffering deeply still;
for Afghanistan, bombed to bits;
for your church in Pakistan, meeting in the shadow of the gun;
even for the terrorists, that they might be brought to justice,
and some day, somehow, from someone, seek and find forgiveness like
Saul of old. Could you make that happen, Lord? Could you?

'Angels in the rafters'

Murree Christian School lay north of Islamabad, Pakistan's stylish capital. Most of the students were the children of missionaries. On August 5, 2002 several fundamentalist Moslem gunmen entered the campus and shot indiscriminately anyone they saw. They peppered the buildings with bullets. Some staff members were killed or wounded. Miraculously not one single student was hurt.

As the children crouched together under desks for safety, some sang faith choruses softly to keep up their spirits and to comfort others. Some spoke aloud in prayer. One small boy prayed aloud for the terrorists themselves – gracious praying, instinctive praying.

Russell Morton, the school Director, has written as follows in *Angels in the Rafters* (Chiang Mai, Thailand, MCS, 2002): 'The school is built into a huge, deconsecrated British garrison church. Some classrooms are four levels up in the towering structure, amid the massive timber rafters. Some students who spent a very long hour hiding in rooms on the upper floors during the attack heard singing coming from above them. "There must have been angels in the rafters," one said. There were.'

Appendix

Reproduced below are three Salvation Army official statements about the war in Iraq. They were issued independently (and apparently without inter-territorial consultation) in the three countries (the USA, Australia, and the UK) that took an active military part in invading Iraq in 2003. The American statement declines to endorse the military action by the USA government and takes a politically neutral position. The Australian statement calls for an outright rejection of the military invasion option over Iraq. The UK statement is more open to military action than the others, but rejects an invasion without the authority of the United Nations.

Hope, Strength, Love
(USA War Cry, April 26, 2003)

The Salvation Army is committed to our troops and their families and will serve them in a variety of ways. We encourage our constituents to pray for wisdom for world leaders and for peace in all nations around the world.

In these troubling times, we urge all Christians and especially all Salvationists to pray that God will intervene in the hearts and thoughts of leaders to find means for a quick and peaceful solution to the conflict that faces our nation and the world. The Salvation Army does not take a political stance on war and will remain neutral in that regard.

Salvationists are urged to pray for our president and for those who provide him with counsel and advice. We are prepared to offer assistance, both practical and spiritual, to those affected directly and indirectly by the war. The Salvation Army is currently providing services to families of military personnel who have been adversely affected by the present situation.

By holding prayer vigils, sending care packages to soldiers leaving for the front lines, and providing physical, emotional and spiritual comfort to families and loved ones left behind, The Salvation Army is dedicated to bringing hope, strength and love during these trying times. The Salvation Army is also prepared to respond to any crisis that may arise at home.

The Salvation Army's views of how Australia should respond to international terrorism
(Australia Southern Territory web site, 21 October 2002)

The recent bombings in Bali are an example of yet another country where terrorism is present. The fact that Australians have suffered dreadful death and injury from these bombings, just as we did in New York in September last year, demonstrates how terrorism is of concern to Australia, wherever it occurs in the world.

Australia should be doing all she can to combat this very real threat. However, this does not include destroying nations that could be viewed as the place terrorists come from, if those nations are prepared to do all they can to bring terrorists to justice.

The continual refusal by Iraq to honour the pledges she made at the conclusion of her eviction from Kuwait is a cause of great concern. We earnestly hope that the endeavours being made by the United Nations to ensure that inspections of potential sites that could produce weapons of mass destruction prove successful. We believe force should only be used to ensure the UN are able to access all areas of Iraq that could be viewed as storage or manufacturing centres for these weapons, if permission is not granted by Iraq.

The recent progress being made to ensure agreement between permanent members of the UN Security Council and Iraq is very encouraging and we hope a strong UN inspection team that is unfettered will stop all talk of a unilateral declaration of war by the USA and the UK, supported by Australia.

However, if all these efforts come to nought, then we call on the Australian government to refrain from endorsing unilateral action, and to continue to use diplomatic means to ensure that war is not started by western countries that still acknowledge a Christian ethic as a keystone of our laws and way of life.

Whatever the provocation, we must never turn away from the vision of an order based on international law instead of the unilateral use of force by a group of countries acting outside the UN and international law.

Statement on the situation in Iraq by The Salvation Army in the United Kingdom with the Republic of Ireland (United Kingdom Territory web site, January 2003)

The Salvation Army in the United Kingdom and Republic of Ireland is very concerned about the situation in Iraq and, like all responsible organisations, thinks that war should always be a last resort. We acknowledge that in some cases war is the lesser of two evils, but we urge world leaders to strive for a peaceful solution to the present crisis.

As an international organisation working in 109 countries, The Salvation Army is well placed to gauge tensions and feelings about a possible conflict with Iraq. Salvationists in the UK would encourage actions and statements showing that a conflict would not be a 'war on Islam'. There is a real fear that Moslem communities in this country and Christian minorities in Moslem countries will be targets for reprisals by extremists. Strong political leadership is required to ensure this does not happen.

It is important in frenzied times that due process is followed and The Salvation Army urges all world leaders to work through the United Nations. If ultimately diplomacy fails and it is proven beyond doubt that Iraq has been harbouring weapons of mass destruction, we hope that any military action would be authorised by the United Nations.

All wars are, in themselves, terrible and destructive events and it is the innocent who suffer most. In the event of war in Iraq, The Salvation Army calls on all sides to do everything in their power to ensure that innocent people are protected. The Iraqi people need our help, that is for certain, and we would not wish to minimise the overwhelming deficiencies of the present Iraqi regime. However, outside assistance must not be prefaced by bombing that wantonly endangers civilian life.

The Salvation Army is aware of the magnitude of the decisions facing world leaders at the moment and calls on all Salvationists, fellow Christians, and people of faith to remember those leaders in their thoughts and prayers in the coming months.

CHAPTER 6

'Partner' or spouse?

Holiness and Cohabiting without Marriage

A choice many will face

HETEROSEXUAL love is a key part of God's plan for the human race. It is important to stress this because the church has not always seen it that way. Sex and sexuality were once regarded only as necessary evils. They proved useful for procreating the species, but were not for indulgence or celebration, and it was definitely not the done thing to speak of pleasure in sex.

Chapter 3 has explored the nature of erotic heterosexual love in the overall context of the love of God (*agape*) and as part of the holy life. It also teased out the biblical basis for marriage and for the non-indulgence by Christians in pre-marital or extra-marital sex.

This essay seeks to examine the phenomenon of couples who cohabit without marriage. In western societies this is now a very widespread practice, no longer frowned upon by society in general. However, those of us who follow the teachings of the Scriptures on marriage (again see Chapter 3 above), and who testify to the blessing of a clean heart, cannot give our approval or encouragement to this choice of lifestyle, however common it may have become or however much we understand the motives of the parties. Modern secular research reinforces the biblical teaching, a fact not often stated or widely known.

Most young people therefore (and not a few older persons too) will face the choice these days: to take a 'partner' or to marry a spouse? Cohabitation as though married, or the real thing – marriage itself?

An increasing trend

Cohabitation refers to a heterosexual couple not formally married to each other living in a domestic relationship of sexual intimacy under the same roof. This occurs in a variety of scenarios. Usually neither of the parties has been married, but sometimes one or both have been divorced and so cohabitation can occur either before or after marriage.

Recent decades have seen a dramatic rise in the number of those cohabiting. Some say that the trend is so strong that it can never be turned round again. If indeed it is incontrovertible, then Christians are going to find themselves always in a minority who reject cohabitation as an option. We live in a time when the church needs to reinforce articulately and persuasively its teaching on marriage and when believers are being called to role model the holy life insofar as it relates to marriage and sexual relations in general.

Let us take the North American scene. Until the mid-1990's many states in the USA still had laws declaring cohabitation for the unmarried illegal. This means that American statistics must be treated with caution since many cohabiting couples kept their status secret for fear of legal repercussions. Official figures, however, show a tripling in the number cohabiting between 1970 and 1980, rising to a total of 1.5 million couples. Between 1980 and 1990 a further increase of 80% took place, making a total of 2.9 million couples. It is estimated that the real total in 1990 is more likely to have been as high as 8 million. The decade ending in 1990 saw a drop in the number of people marrying but no increase in the total of single persons. This is explained by the increased popularity of cohabitation. A similar upsurge has been seen in Canada where cohabitation was little known prior to the 1970's but where the 1981 census reported over 700,000 cohabiting couples. This rose to 1.4 million by 1991, or 10% of all couples.

Research in the United Kingdom, France, Switzerland, Denmark and the Netherlands shows that Europe experienced the same swift increase in those choosing a cohabiting lifestyle. It was little different in New Zealand and Australia.

Why cohabit?

It is vital that those seeking a sanctified mind on this issue understand the factors that drove such a marked change. In all the countries mentioned above two features appeared in common. One was the introduction of the contraceptive pill. The other was the steady liberalisation of abortion laws. These had the combined effect of promoting more and more sexual relations outside marriage.

A greater number of women also wanted to follow professional careers and this, combined with the two factors already mentioned, made cohabitation a preferred option over marriage. Cohabiting was (at first, but not now) perceived as an extension of courtship. Add to this the liberalisation also of divorce laws in western legal systems, and the negative imaging of marriage was complete. It was needed less and less by women as a means of subsistence due to their growing economic independence and a corresponding diminishing need of a husband for fiscal or material support.

Many commentators highlight also the growing individualism of the western world during and after the 1960's. This has seen the gradual but ineluctable replacing of a 'we' culture by a 'me' culture. Personal choice has come to take priority over the interests of a spouse, of family, or of one's social group. Cohabitation is one result of this major shift in western social attitudes during the twentieth century. One leading British politician has spoken of 'the *self-first* disease which is debasing British society'. This might be said of western society in general. The growth of a 'consumer culture' seems to have reinforced an ethos of individual choice. Christians know that without the grace of God people with freedom to choose almost always choose selfishly. This is the opposite of sanctified choosing. The Spirit-filled life places others at the heart of things.

Any consideration of the reasons for the emergence of cohabiting in recent years cannot ignore the demise in Christian convictions throughout western countries. Cohabitation is more likely to occur where religious belief is weak. One study in the USA (1987-8 National Survey of Families and Households) found that 'persons with no religious preference have a much higher approval of cohabiting than any of the other groups.' Christian groups most likely to approve of cohabitation were Episcopalians, followed by Roman Catholics and Presbyterians. The same survey showed that those attending church weekly were over three times less likely to cohabit than those attending only monthly. Research in the United Kingdom produced similar results.

Mention needs to be made of the negative image of marriage that has been promoted intentionally by some in recent years. This too has encouraged cohabitation, falsely idealised as liberation from the so-called constraints of patriarchal marriage. A survey in the USA in 1997 of twenty undergraduate textbooks on marriage and the family concluded that the books 'convey a determinedly pessimistic view of marriage'. They left out the advantages of marriage and highlighted its challenges. Most of the books surveyed 'short-changed children, devoting far more pages to adult problems than to issues concerning child wellbeing.'

A prelude to marriage?

Cohabiting is generally assumed to be a *pre*-nuptial state. That is to say, it is often taken for granted it will lead on into marriage sooner or later for the couple. This is a mistaken view. Contrary to popular opinion, cohabiting is not mainly a prelude to marriage. Many couples enter it seeking only a *non*-nuptial relationship. Cohabitors are just as likely to return to singleness as to enter into marriage. In the USA 66% of all cohabiting relationships in the 1980's ended before two years had elapsed, and 40% of these ended, not by marriage, but by the parties abandoning the relationship entirely.

Many couples who cohabit never have plans to marry. For them the cohabiting was never a 'trial marriage' (see below) or a prelude to marriage. It was simply an alternative to marriage. The possibility of marrying was either never contemplated or, if it was, it was deliberately rejected. One American researcher found cohabiting to be 'an ephemeral pairing based on sexual attraction' and a bypassing of marriage 'without loss of a convenient sexual partnership'. Readers will see at once how far this is at variance with the Bible's view of the place of marriage. It ranks cohabiting, in terms of honourable intentions, alongside adultery or the keeping of mistresses.

'Trial marriage'?

While many choosing to cohabit do so to compare cohabiting, not with marriage, but with living singly, some do in fact still use it to attempt what is called a 'trial marriage'. This concept has become very plausible indeed, but it is based on obviously false logic. A couple may be heard to say that the high divorce rate was a cause for concern and that they did not wish to end up in the divorce courts. They might believe that living together first to test compatibility is a sensible option. So plausible is this view that in the early 1990's a clear majority of American young people agreed with the statement that 'it is usually a good idea for a couple to live together before getting married in order to find out whether they really get along.' The only good thing about this view is that it hints at a desire for marriages, once entered upon, to endure.

The whole idea of the trial marriage is blown apart by the plain fact that, according to research evidence from several countries, those who cohabit before marriage have a higher risk (in Canada the risk is doubled) of eventually being divorced. The low commitment / high autonomy attitude found in a cohabitation can get carried over into the marriage. The marriages of serial cohabitors are especially at risk.

A moment's thought will show that a person cannot possibly experience what marriage is like without actually being married. A trial marriage is a myth. It cannot exist. At the heart of marriage is an unconditional, mutual and public commitment between a man and a woman for life, to the exclusion of all others in terms of covenantal relationship. Marriage rests on the principles of reliability, continuity and availability. In a 'trial marriage' all these are explicitly compromised and conditional. To experience what marriage is like, you have to be married. Cohabiting is a false test. You may as well speak of 'trial conversion' to see what accepting Jesus is like!

More facts about cohabitation

Research in Britain, with results echoed in the USA, indicates that cohabitation has weakened the connection between marriage and parenting. There have been two huge changes in the last thirty years with regard to reproductive behaviour: the separation of sexual intercourse from marriage; the separation of marriage from parenthood.

Back in the 1960's, when an unmarried couple conceived, they married. Today they are more likely to get an abortion or simply go for an illegitimate birth. Cohabitation is locked into the decline of marriage and also into the sharp rise in childbirth outside marriage. Cohabiting has increased the number of abortions.

Cohabiting has lessened the degree of commitment men make to women. This is a bad deal for women. The substitution of cohabitation for marriage is a story, first and foremost, of lower commitment by women to men, but – significantly – even lower still commitment by men to women. This in turn has led to what has been called 'a retreat from children' since men increasingly view children and fatherhood primarily as responsibility and obligation rather than as a source of happiness and family stability.

A sampling of 13,000 people in the USA in 1987-8 compared the quality of relationships in marriage with those in cohabiting lifestyles. Couples in cohabiting unions were found to have poorer relationships compared with those within marriages. The differences became clearest when the incidence of domestic violence was compared. Even after allowing for education, race, age and gender, pre-nuptial cohabitors (those planning one day to marry) were 1.8 times more likely to engage in domestic violence, while the non-nuptial couples (those not contemplating marriage) were exactly twice (2.0) as likely to suffer violence from a partner.

Impacts of cohabitation on children

There is mounting and compelling evidence that cohabitation is a bad deal, not only for women, but for children too. Research into non-marital pregnancies has traditionally focussed on births to single mothers. More recent work has now included births to cohabiting mothers, or previously cohabiting mothers, and this shows a high increase in births to a single parent due to cohabiting. In 50% of cases, a man will exit a cohabiting relationship when a pregnancy occurs. This is especially so where there has been an understanding of 'no children', or where the onset of the pregnancy is seen as an attempt to trap a man into marriage. In the United Kingdom about 40% of one-parent families emerge from a failed cohabiting union. Figures for the USA are similar. Over 75% of American children born to cohabiting parents will see their parents split up before they reach sixteen. The percentage falls to only 33% for children born within marriage. This is still alarmingly high, but the deprivation risk to children born to cohabitors is much, much worse.

Children born to cohabitors will also be poorer than children born to married parents. USA research in 1996 showed that the poverty rate for children within marriages was 6%, while for those in cohabiting unions (a total of 2.2 million children) it was 31%. The rate for those living with a single parent was 45%.

Just as cohabiting couples are more likely to be violent to one another than married couples, so too children of cohabitors are more likely to suffer abuse – 20 times more likely – than those having married parents. The likelihood of abuse rises to a multiplier of 33 for children living with their mother and a man who is not their father. This is both the worst and the commonest scenario of all for children in cohabiting couple households. By sharp contrast, the best chance of happiness for a child is to be born to a married couple who love each other.

A bad deal

'Partner' or spouse? A cohabiting 'partner' is not a spouse in God's eyes, but a spouse is a partner in the deepest possible sense, and a Christian spouse is a co-seeker after holiness of life. In contrast, cohabitation has been proven by research to be bad for those choosing it (both male and female), damaging to children (including the unborn), and a danger to the interests of women. It is, ironically, today's greatest threat to our search for true intimacy. Little wonder the Scriptures, and the way of holiness, turn away from it.

CHAPTER 7

WRITING IN THE DUST

HOLINESS AND LEADERSHIP PRINCIPLES FROM SCRIPTURE

Secular and ecclesiastical leadership

L EADERSHIP is a word on everyone's lips these days, or so it seems. It has superseded 'management'. We exhausted management, so now we have leadership. The received wisdom today is that skilled managers, once revered and valued, are not enough. It is leaders we need. Leaders are not mere managers (but how I thank God for skilled managers within the Body of Christ).

Constantly our attention is drawn to leadership in corporate circles, and occasionally some entrepreneur emerges from the world of big business, with all its pressures and profit motives, to be held out before us as an icon, a leader to be admired. We are told by the PR people and the spin doctors that he or she is no mere manager, but a great leader of vision and thrust, inspiring all around to more and more productivity, creative effort and higher earnings.

This archetypal commercial leader is not only a change bringer, but also an anticipator of societal and economic trends. He is a seer no less, a prophet, a worker of miracles. No sooner has he made his name, than he becomes a writer of axiomatic, definitive, best-selling, and occasionally over-hyped books on leadership principles and techniques. He is paid vast sums to be an after dinner speaker on leadership, and after that he founds his very own Leadership Institute, with membership mainly by correspondence, but – naturally – for a fee. If we join, he will mail us tapes accompanied by notes so that even we can understand something of his often witty, but always profound utterances, though somehow we shall never quite aspire to reach his great and lofty corporate height.

Needless to say, not everyone is excited by such a picture.

Does the corporate world truly have apt role models for spiritual and ecclesiastical leadership? It does indeed have fine people, gifted people, impressive in their wealth-creating abilities. We can learn from their single-mindedness and energy. Many corporate leaders are also committed Christians. However, for the timeless, essential maxims of spiritual leadership within the church, within the Body of Christ, within

God's Salvation Army, we must be willing to look elsewhere. It is from the Bible that we must search out the shape of holy, sanctified leadership. Indeed, it is my conviction that the flow of ideas and principles needs to be reversed, so that instead of the corporate world influencing the Body, we should seek to have God's timeless leadership principles, which we can mine and extract from the rich deposits of His timeless Scriptures, take root and thereby influence secular spheres like the market place and the office.

Old and New Testaments

The aim of this essay is to draw out key leadership principles as they apply to the holy work of leading the people of God. Two compelling, dramatic Bible narratives will be used: 1 Samuel 3:1-19 which recounts the divine call of young Samuel into leadership; and then John 7:53-8:11 in which we see Jesus Himself exercising leadership skills as the woman caught in adultery is dragged before Him in the Temple precincts in Jerusalem. These narratives are set centuries apart, but taken together they afford a unique opportunity to tease out eternal leadership principles for sanctified leaders. (At this point readers should turn to the two Bible references.)

Each leadership principle will be denoted by the abbreviation 'LP' followed by a number for ease of future reference or discussion. The principles enunciated are by no means exhaustive and are not intended as the last word on Christian leadership. They are offered merely as a potentially helpful and thought-provoking contribution toward sanctified leadership at any level within the Body of Christ.

The Calling by God of Samuel to be a Leader (1 Samuel 3:1-19)

It was a spiritually barren time. There had been no word or vision from the Lord. Samuel was born into this setting. We do not know Samuel's age. Tradition has him at about twelve, but we could also think of him as in his early teens. The Hebrew text is not clear on this. All we know is that he was young. Also in the narrative is Eli who was old and virtually blind. Eli is the leader, to our eyes. Young Samuel was not ready.

LP 1: Sanctified, spiritual leadership is not always marked by inspirational vision or prophetic utterance.

This is a vital thing to understand. It is true for the vast majority of spiritual leaders. God does not require brilliance. He does not demand that we develop a high personal profile. However, He does require sanctity and faithfulness in a leader. Eli was such a one. His public leadership (as distinct from the problems of his family life) was unspectacular, but faithful. He was a holy and godly leader, and yet had known no vision or prophetic gift. Many in leadership today can take heart from this.

LP 2: A sanctified leader must have a quiet place where all noises, other than God's voice, will be stilled.

Look at the timing of God's call to Samuel. It was just before the dawn. The Almighty chose pre-dawn when all other voices and clamour were stilled. Snatching a moment in the car, at the airport, in the plane etc. might help but it is not enough. Absolute, physical quiet is the absolutely best setting for the hearing of God's voice. God's leader needs to have such a place into which to withdraw from the clamour of the world. A place of retreat, however short. A place of secret prayer. A place of intense listening to, waiting for God. Jesus did this (Luke 6:12-16). He spent a night on a silent hillside before choosing the Twelve.

LP 3: In God's eyes the true leader may not be the leader according to human eyes.

When we read these verses we think Eli is the leader. So he is. But there is a second leader and this is Samuel. We are dealing with two leaders here.

When God decided to break the divine silence into which Samuel had been born, and through which Eli had lived and led, He bypassed the senior leadership and spoke instead directly to a young fellow who was not at all ready according to received human wisdom. He was a juvenile, untrained, a novice. He did not know the Lord or the ways of the Lord, but he had a huge capacity for sanctity.

What lessons are there for us in this? What does it say to us about the way we see our younger staff, younger officers, newly commissioned officers, the youth in the Army? Perhaps we are tempted to view them only as potential leaders, when all along God sees them as leaders now. Sanctified leadership is not the exclusive prerogative of the middle-aged or elderly.

LP 4: A sanctified leader has to be in the right place to hear God's message.

Samuel was in the sanctuary, surrounded by the sacred things of the Lord. He slumbered in the tranquillity of the Temple precinct.

God's little leader was in the right place to hear, but we know that God could have reached him anywhere. Still, it is good he was positioned to hear. I think of my children. We have three. We have tried to give them latitude in this modern age, but we have always had ground rules for them. One of them was that while they lived under the same roof as their folks they would attend the house of God at least once every Sunday. We wanted them to be positioned to hear God's voice. We wanted them to be in the sanctuary, though we knew God could reach them wherever they might be. We reckoned the chances were better if they were surrounded by the sacred things of God and by God's people, even if they did not at that time give a profound inner assent to the gospel of Jesus Christ. We wanted them to be ready to respond, in case in God's eyes one or more of them was to be a leader for Him one day, and in case God could see in them a greater capacity for holiness than could we, their parents.

LP 5: A sanctified leader needs to know the difference between God's voice and merely human voices.

Samuel was not yet schooled in this art. It takes time, but is an integral part of growing within the holy life. Samuel had an excuse. What about you and me? Do we know the difference? Are we knowledgeable in how God speaks? Have we matured in our grasp of how God guides? Do we realise that it is common for the Tempter to disguise his voice as that of an angel? The true, sanctified leader for God must learn how to test the many voices that clamour for attention.

LP 6: A sanctified leader enjoys God's patience.

Even seasoned leaders can be slow to catch on to the plan of God. Here Eli took three times to get the point. God did not mind. Divine patience is extended toward a faithful, if unspectacular, holy leader. Already we have noted that God requires faithfulness and a holy walk, not brilliance.

It also follows that, if God extends patience to the leader, the leader must extend patience to those led, especially when they fail to grasp the message or the vision. There will come a point when some will have to be left behind, but meanwhile a leader is to make every possible effort to carry the judgement of those being led.

LP 7: Senior spiritual leaders need to give constant encouragement to younger spiritual leaders.

Eli gave Samuel very clear and straightforward guidance. He told him what to do and what to say. Clear guidance is a key form of encouragement. It is also a form of sound pastoral care (a thing we need to re-emphasise and re-capture these days). A sanctified senior leader will never feel threatened by a gifted younger leader. If both are close to God, the benefit will be to the Kingdom, and thus to both of them.

LP 8: Sometimes a spiritual leader will be visited by God.

This happened to Samuel. 'The Lord came and stood there' (verse 10). Both Old Testament and New Testament have many other instances of this. God stood there 'calling'. When He comes, He speaks, and when He speaks He usually calls. A sanctified, spiritual leader must be ready for such a visitation by God. Read again the prayer poems of the French priest Michel Quoist and sense the wonder of this happening, even amid the busy traffic of Paris! We need to note also that no such visit was paid to Eli. Yet his public leadership was profoundly faithful. The only blot on the landscape for Eli was his failure with his own family.

LP 9: God may require His chosen, sanctified leader to speak a terrible, tragic message.

Spiritual leadership is not all privilege. It is not for popularity. We do not do it in order to be liked. It is mostly burden. Sometimes even novice leaders can be asked by God to undertake something terrible. The task can be daunting. It can be one from which we shrink. Let us notice carefully that God was willing to entrust to the novice, Samuel, something that few human leaders – however godly – would have asked him to do. God will often entrust to younger leaders much more than their human, sensible, cautious senior leaders would give them. God sees their capacities and their readiness even – perhaps especially – when we do not.

LP 10: It is OK for a sanctified leader to be scared, provided fear is accompanied by obedience.

Samuel was scared (verse 15). Of course, he was scared! He was about to tell his boss the last thing the boss wanted to hear! Do you know that feeling?

It is OK for a sanctified leader to be nervous, apprehensive or even plain afraid, provided this is overcome in obedience to the command of the Lord. At the very heart of the holy life lies obedience to the divine will. The message must be spoken. The word must be delivered. God's leader will be given God's holy courage to speak the message, plus God's holy wisdom on how to speak it. Obedience to God must outweigh fear of man.

LP 11: Younger leaders ought not to underestimate the spiritual resilience of older leaders.

In Samuel's very human and understandable fear there was as much fear for Eli as for himself. It was, if you like, a selfless fear. He was afraid for Eli. Well, on this occasion the younger leader underestimated the capacities of the senior leader. The godly Eli refused to hide from the truth (verse 17). He did not like it when he heard it, but to his eternal credit he took it as from the Lord. In so doing, he honoured the Lord and honoured his younger eventual successor also.

LP 12: A sanctified leader must be ready to hand over power.

The events we have read paved the way for a much-needed hand over of power. The best leaders are leaders who, under God, prepare from day one of assuming office to transfer power to an eventual successor. This is sanctified common sense. It is God's authority we wield, and to cling to it too long is a sin. If we find ourselves loving the power we exercise, it is time to step into the background and make way for another.

Let us now move on through many centuries to join Jesus in Jerusalem and to witness an extraordinary event, one that has haunted readers of the Bible for 2000 years. From the narrative found in the Fourth Gospel we can extract still further timeless principles for sanctified leadership in the church.

The Woman taken in Adultery (John 7:53-8:11)

Here we are handling one of the most riveting narratives of the entire

Scriptures. It is an account (I do not say 'story' since that word carries overtones of fiction) of the woman who was caught in an adulterous encounter and dragged in front of Jesus.

Before enunciating further timeless principles of spiritual leadership found in these verses, let us note the following pivotal facts:

1. Here we have many leaders, but just one victim.
2. All the leaders are male.
3. The sad, solitary, sin-stained victim is female.
4. Her partner in adultery, by definition male, is never mentioned. Where was he? Who was he?
5. These events, like Samuel's call, also take place at dawn, in the stillness. However, this time there is brittle ugliness when the shrill, accusing voices break in upon the measured, reasoned voice of Jesus as He teaches in the Temple.
6. The adultery has taken place during the night. A dawn raid on the house has produced one of the culprits. While the raid took place, Jesus was teaching quietly in the Temple. A crowd was there. At dawn, so early? Yes. In Lahore, Pakistan where we lived for nearly five years, at dawn the parks are thronged with people seeking cool air before the sun comes up to scorch the earth accompanied by humidity such as would stifle your every breath. Jerusalem would have been like that. It was one of the reasons the Romans dreaded a posting to Judea or its environs.

LP 13: Genuine spiritual leaders do not always match the facile, modern stereotypes.

The first leader to appear in this episode is Jesus. He did not look like a typical leader. He had simplicity of dress, no wealth, no position, no office, no power-base, and no organisation behind him. He was taken more as a teacher than as a leader in the eyes of the people. When eventually the people recognised Him as a genuine leader, the transition proved fatal. Saying 'yes' to the Father's will and stepping into leadership for God can cost you dearly in this world. Disobedience can cost much more.

LP 14: Some who look like godly leaders are in fact wolves in sheep's clothing.

Jesus spoke openly of this – see John 10. As Jesus taught in the Temple, the scribes (NIV: 'teachers of the law', that is, specialists in the religious law codes of Moses) and the Pharisees entered the scene. They looked on the surface like real spiritual leaders. They were recognised by everyone as spiritual leaders. This is what gave them their identity and purpose in life. Yet they were not the real thing. Compared with Jesus they were wolves dressed as sheep and they were intent on attacking the flock (see again John 10). Outwardly they looked the part. They had special uniforms, with special braid and tassels. Let us be warned again that outward garb is no qualification. The only Real Leader there was Jesus, in his common, crumpled clothing.

The saddest, most alarming thing of all was that the scribes and Pharisees did not know that they were not true spiritual leaders. This made them especially dangerous, for they were cocksure of their rightness. Humility of mind, or readiness to learn, was absent. The possibility of being wrong simply did not enter their frame of reference. In doing evil they genuinely thought they were doing good. Jesus came to change all that.

LP 15: Sanctified leaders will take care not to abuse their powers.

The religious leaders of the Jews brought with them a victim. She was female. All her accusers were male. Her male co-sinner, her fellow-adulterer had been let go. She was an easy victim.

It is the greatest temptation of those with power to produce victims in order to prove their power. True spiritual leaders do not do this. They should have no victims. Abuse of spiritual power is the worst abuse. Corruption of the best is the worst corruption.

LP 16: A sanctified leader knows that all leadership power, including power within the Body of Christ, is addictive.

The Pharisees, addicted to power and control of others, were not satisfied with one victim. She was really nothing to them, just a pawn in a bigger game. It was Jesus they were after. He was the big prize. Verse 6 is clear. They were intent on entrapment. He was good, but they thought of him as evil. They were evil, but they sincerely thought themselves good. Two victims would be better than one. It would prove they were doubly effective. Having tasted blood, their appetites were whetted for another attack. They were addicted. Sanctified leaders do not leave a trail of victims in their wake.

LP 17: Behavioural conformity is not a prerequisite of spiritual leadership.

Jesus, the Real Leader, behaved oddly. He wrote ciphers in the sand. Why? What did He write? What was He doing? Why be enigmatic?

What lessons does this bring to us? None. Jesus is unique. Centuries later we still do not know what He was doing. He is 'Mystery'. He is 'The Unfathomable'. Let those of us who model ourselves upon Him, note only that we need not fear if we are sometimes deemed eccentric in His service. Let us throw off forever the straitjacket of the world's behaviour code.

LP 18: Sanctified leaders must be ready to confront the powers of darkness.

Suddenly we find Jesus is up on His feet, feet soon to be – but not yet – nailed down. He is standing up, and 'standing up to' them. He is no longer avoiding a direct encounter of the eyes. He is speaking to them face to face. His voice rings out in challenge. 'If you are pure, throw the first stone.' The Real Leader has, in a single sentence, shifted the focus of attention from the solitary, shamed woman to her accusers. Now all eyes are on the men of power and influence. They have been exposed by the Lord's confronting of them. It is their turn to be judged, impostor leaders that they are. Not one of them is 'without sin', and this fact is out in the open. Jesus had made sure of it.

LP 19: Sanctified leaders function not only in their local setting, but also in a global and eternal context.

Once more, a second time, Jesus is writing on the ground. He is 'Mystery' again, with universal dimensions. Martin Luther King has written of his constant sense of 'cosmic companionship'. If true for him, then how much more for Jesus, Son of God. If I were forced to hazard the meaning of His actions I would side with the Japanese theologian, Kosuke Koyama. Jesus was tapping shoulders. His finger outstretched, He tapped shoulders. He was tapping your shoulder, my shoulder. He was tapping the shoulder of all the world, the shoulder of the planet, of the entire universe, and He was saying: 'Come near. Listen to what I am about to say. Look upon what I am about to do. Bear witness. Come and see, come and hear, come and never forget.' The whole universe needed to know and to see this thing that was about to pass. It was something of cosmic proportions. It had eternal dimensions, and foreshadowed the ultimate benefits of the Cross.

LP 20: Sanctified leaders transform victims into victors.

This happens by the grace and power of God. Here Jesus gifted this woman, a hapless victim of false leaders, with dignity and respect. He was gentle with her, sensitive to her gender, her shame, her social lot, and her need of forgiveness and healing. He was, to her, the 'Perfect Answer'. He held out to her health and healing and wholeness such as she had never known could exist. He met her in her fullness of need. It was full salvation.

She had encountered sanctity in *the* sanctified leader. His divine, sublime words, words of strong mercy and strong doctrine, ring in our ears today. He spoke them to her, and He speaks them still to us, to me: 'Neither do I condemn you. Go now and leave your life of sin.'

[*Note 1*: A modified version of this essay was first prepared for the Canada and Bermuda Territory's 'Mission Without Borders' Conference, Mississauga, Ontario – Welcome Banquet Plenary Session, 25 October 2001.
Note 2: See also Chapter 12 in which Commissioner Joe Noland writes challengingly about biblical role models for leadership in the church.]

PART
TWO

CHAPTER 8

GRACE, ELOQUENCE AND POWER

HOLINESS AND THE USE OF WORDS

Lt. Colonel Marlene Chase

Like a human soul, a word, once born can never be aborted.
Bring it safe, holy Midwife, to reflect the face of God.

JEWISH wisdom tradition considers that words have 'being'. They take on an existence which, when spoken, cannot be revoked. The Word of God has a life of its own, and everything hangs together because of the *Logos* – Jesus Christ of whom Scripture records, 'No one ever spoke like this Man' (John 7:46). This same Jesus is with us even now as we share His living word with the world.

Our faith is not a matter of simply hearing what Christ said long ago and trying to carry it out. Rather, in the words of C.S. Lewis, 'The real Son of God is at your side. He is beginning to turn you into the same kind of thing as Himself. He is beginning, so to speak, to 'inject' His kind of life and thought, His *zoe* (life), into you; beginning to turn the tin soldier into a live man. The part of you that does not like it is the part that is still tin.'

The evangelical tradition of Christianity is founded upon the proclaimed and written Word of God as incarnated in Jesus Christ, the Living Word. Jesus told His followers, 'When the Holy Spirit comes on you ... you will be my witnesses ... to the ends of the earth' (Acts 1:8). 'A witness ... can no longer be his own master,' writes Karl Barth. 'He is constrained to obey. Whenever we make our own ideas our theme and subject, our testimony is no longer pure.' Like David, the disciple's heart can be 'stirred by a noble theme' and all our words be 'verses for the King' (Psalm 45:1).

The word, *logos*, was understood by the Greeks as denoting the unifying, rational principle that held the world together. They also understood it as the natural law that people had of necessity to live by. Word and reason – these two are always intertwined. But in Jewish thought a word was more than a sound expressing a meaning; a word actually did things. God's word is not simply sound; it is cause. The Jews used the term to signify the instrument by which the world was created. 'By the word of the Lord the heavens were made ... for he spoke and it came to be; he commanded, and it stood firm' (Psalm 33:6,9).

John identifies Christ as the divine *Logos* – the Word – by whom the world was made, who became flesh to enable people to become children of God (John 1:1).

A holy purpose

It is with our words, emanating from a holy life, that we testify of Christ and His Kingdom. 'As the heavens are higher than the earth, so are my ways higher than your ways and my thoughts than your thoughts,' God says. 'As the rain and the snow come down from heaven, and do not return to it without watering the earth and making it bud and flourish, so that it yields seed for the sower and bread for the eater, so is my word that goes out from my mouth: It will not return to me empty, but will accomplish what I desire and achieve the purpose for which I sent it' (Isaiah 55: 9-11).

Our tongues were created for a holy purpose – to praise God and bless people. Yet, too few Christians take seriously enough this sacred purpose for speech. We would never think of committing physical murder, but we have sometimes committed verbal manslaughter, allowing ourselves to be caught up in things God hates. It is interesting to note that of the seven things God hates as listed in Proverbs 6, three have to do with speech: 'lying lips, false witness and the spreading of strife'.

Because of the impact of language on our lives, there is no such thing as mere rhetoric. Everything we say is important and has consequences. We shall be held responsible for our words as well as for our deeds. We who have embarked upon the life of a disciple – someone who is *with* Jesus, learning to be *like* Him – find the tongue the hardest to control of all our members. 'Out of the same mouth come praise and cursing!' observed the Apostle James. 'My brothers, this should not be' (James 3:9). James clearly makes controlling the tongue the touchstone of disciplined living: 'If any man offend not in word, the same is a perfect man, and able also to bridle the whole body' (3:2). Though this passage holds particular instruction for pastors, teachers and church leaders, it is important for all of us.

Those who give leadership to the people of God have always held an important place in the Scriptures and were held in high esteem. In the Old Testament, prophets and kings handed down the whole story of Israel, but their significant place shifted largely to teachers in the New Testament. Jesus was known as *Rabbi* (literally 'Great One') or Teacher by His followers.

In the early church, written documents were extremely rare and unavailable to the masses. The spoken word was the major means of transmitting ideas, and it fell to teachers to transmit accurately the Christian faith. It is not hard to understand how error could enter the church. No wonder James counsels, 'Not many of you should presume to be teachers, my brothers, because you know that we who teach will be judged more strictly' (3:1). Notably, James includes himself in that judgement. He was not referring to the school teaching profession, but rather was emphasising the crucial role of teaching spiritual truth. Jesus Himself condemned anyone who led 'little ones' astray (Matthew 18: 6-7).

'I preach, I teach, I counsel using words,' says Eugene Peterson in *Living the Message*. 'People often pay particular attention on the chance that God may be using my words to speak to them. I have a responsibility to use words accurately and well. But it isn't easy. I live in a world where words are used carelessly by some, cunningly by others.'

Discipline and the Word

Discipline can never be a substitute for holiness, but there is interaction between the two. Entire sanctification is the secret of successful Christian discipline, and maintaining discipline is a necessary aid in maintaining holiness. When the Spirit breaks down our stony hearts, we will adjust to the idea of discipline with a new humility and teachability. Indeed, we will long for it, for the desire to be like our Lord will be strong within us.

'Out of the abundance of the heart, the mouth speaks,' Jesus said, affirming that what we are on the inside will come out in speech and reflect the kind of persons we truly are (Matthew 12:34). James knew that everyone falls short of the mark. 'We all stumble in many ways,' he writes. 'If anyone is never at fault in what he says, he is a perfect man, able to keep his whole body in check' (James 3:2). In all probability, this should not be taken literally (since one could control the tongue and still make mistakes in other ways) but should stand as a proverb emphasising the difficulty, and yet the great importance, of disciplined speech in the Christian's life.

In *The Disciplined Life* Richard Taylor writes: 'Regardless how carefully controlled a person is in all other points, none can qualify for the high rating of a truly disciplined character whose tongue is not restrained by the bridle of prudence and directed by the reins of love.'

Someone has suggested that we are most troubled by our tongues because, of all the parts of the body, it is the easiest to move. Our tongues can move for hours on end, and our bodies will feel no fatigue apart from a slight sore throat after extended speech. It may also be true that of all the spiritual gifts, some are (mistakenly) most intrigued by 'tongues' precisely because of this ease. It would be wonderful if we had only to open our mouths and out would come some heavenly language over which we need have no control. No discipline on our part would be needed, but we find it is not so with our day to day conversation in the home and the market place.

'Two distressing symptoms of the moral deterioration of our generation are the increasing use of vulgar and profane speech and the deliberate cult of obscenity and pornography,' notes the Army's current *Orders and Regulations for Soldiers*. 'These testify to a coarseness and crudity of character which are of grave consequence to the individual and the community. The salvation soldier must beware of the subtle influence of the world in these respects. He must not allow his reactions against vulgarity and swearing in general (particularly in literature and the mass media) to be blunted.'

The dust of the world rubs off on our hands, stings our eyes and ears, blunts our perceptions. It would be wrong to think that because our hearts have been sanctified wholly, therefore whatever we say is holy. To excuse critical, unkind, cutting remarks that hurt others and hinder the work of God by saying, 'God knows my heart is pure,' is a great travesty. The discipline of controlling our speech demands the most diligent attention, for the whisper of the Holy Spirit could be obliterated in the noise of society's grasping after luxury and ease. No boot strap religion is strong enough to control this matter of speech. It takes a renovation from the inside out through the daily active control of the Spirit. Richard Foster reminds us that we cannot *preach* good news and *be* bad news! If we are to be witnesses of the gospel in everyday speech, we will need to stay ever nearer to Jesus so that we keep clear the vision of the sacred Word – and of words – which God has declared shall be holy, even as He is.

The word of fire

James uses three graphic metaphors to explain that small causes may produce large results – bits in horses' mouths, the rudders of ships, and a little flame that kindles a great forest. While it appears at first glance that James is using the metaphor *fire* in a negative sense, followed by 'a world of evil', fire as a picture evokes some strong connections to holiness. 'Our God is a consuming fire' we read in the Pentateuch (Deuteronomy 4:24), and the Holy Spirit is often symbolised in Scripture by fire. John the Baptist said of Jesus, 'He will baptise you with the Holy Spirit and with fire ... that will burn up the chaff with the unquenchable fire' (Matthew 3:11-12). His purpose is to consume the dross of sin and refine the soul to Jesus' likeness.

Moses was confronted by God in the form of a burning bush, and he had to remove his shoes in the presence of the Holy One. When Isaiah saw God 'high and lifted up', his first response was: 'I am a man of unclean lips, and I live among a people of unclean lips' (Isaiah 6:5). The angel brought flaming coals to touch his lips and sanctify him for service.

The Holy Spirit's first touch upon the believers at Pentecost had to do with their tongues. 'There came a sound from heaven as of a rushing mighty wind, and it filled all the house where they were sitting.

And there appeared unto them cloven tongues like as of fire, and it sat upon each of them. And they were all filled with the Holy Ghost and began to speak with other tongues, as the Spirit gave them utterance' (Acts 2:2-4, AV).

When the fire of the Holy Spirit consumes what is unlovely and worthless, He settles on our lives with a steady flame that sweeps across the world with cleansing, renewing fire. Catherine Booth, moved by the urging of the Holy Spirit to speak in His name, had a great preaching ministry. 'Her words made preachers tremble,' wrote one Army historian, Cyril Barnes. 'Businessmen were compelled to look to their sense of values. Inactive professing Christians found a power to make them live. Those who surrendered to the will of God received encouragement and fresh impetus.' During a campaign in the West End of London, she wrote, in a letter to her friend, Mrs. Billups, about the thrill of seeing people come to the Lord: 'The Lord has very graciously stood by me. It seems as though He gave me words of fire for them, and they sat spellbound.' Such was the influence of her fiery words that after the father of Archbishop Davidson had heard Catherine preach in the Exeter Hall, London, he begged his son: 'If ever I am charged with a crime, don't bother to engage any of the great lawyers to defend me; get that woman!'

The right word

'A word aptly spoken is like apples of gold in settings of silver' (Proverbs 25:11).

My 'country aunt' was my favourite when I was a child. Not that her city counterparts were not wonderful people whom I loved, but Aunt Dina embodied a kind of natural beauty and order that I found especially attractive. The time-honoured practice of sitting down to the table at mealtime was a habit she refused to abandon, even in later years when that custom was challenged. With my aunt I associate a white linen tablecloth starched and ironed to perfection, real cloth napkins carefully folded, and clean, sparkling dinnerware. Aunt Dina's table always featured some centerpiece of grace and beauty.

Her favourite was a silver basket-like bowl that she reserved for special occasions. From one of the several fruit trees on the farm she chose five perfect golden apples, polished them with beeswax and placed them artfully in the bowl. The top apple retained a pinkish blush and two or three of its own dark green leaves. The effect was one of simple elegance.

Whether the writer of Proverbs had such a centerpiece in mind when he wrote his delightful simile, one cannot be sure. Jamieson, Fausset and Brown, in their commentary, indicate that such might be the case, or that the writer might have been alluding to imitations on silver embroidery. The image at once summons the idea of beauty and good taste. Coupled with its allusion to the apt word, or 'the word fitly spoken' as the King James Version renders it, the picture engenders some rather significant insights. What is the poet trying to tell us about the 'apt' word? Surely his image is part of his truth. George Eliot, in *Middlemarch*, wrote: 'A poet's ... knowledge passes instantaneously into feeling, and feeling flashes back as a new organ of knowledge.' In this simile feelings and knowledge link to say something important about the spoken word.

The word is the right word to speak because it is the true word. Silver and gold, to which the writer refers, are both precious metals, costly substances that must be refined. The purer the gold or silver, the greater the price. The truth is often costly, but precious and enduring. Recently a reporter for the *New York Times* was fired when it became known that for a period of five years he had invented, falsified or plagiarized news reports, passing them off as fact. The fallout from that kind of blatant irresponsibility with words has yet to be totalled. Imagine then the effect of carelessness and callousness in matters of eternal significance!

For the disciple who follows Christ, the true word is the word that springs from a heart that has been purified through the powerful work of the Holy Spirit. 'Surely you desire truth in the inward parts,' the Psalmist wrote, knowing that the inner part determines the direction of the outward behaviour (Psalm 51:6). Socrates wrote, 'Speak, man, so that I can see you.' Those who hear our words are listening for the cadences of Christ. The Apostle Peter urged, 'If anyone speaks, he should do it as one speaking the very words of God' (1 Peter 4:11).

The comparison with 'apples of gold in settings of silver' immediately evokes a sense of richness. The word aptly spoken enriches both the one who speaks and the one who hears. How often have we been touched by words that illumine, inspire, impel us? Words can lift us to the heights or bring us to the depths. Paul urged Timothy: 'Preach the Word; be prepared in season and out of season' (2 Timothy 4:2) in order to bring enrichment to the souls of others.

The apt word is the beautiful word. The world abounds in careless, ugly, negative words. People who cherish truth heed the injunction of Scripture: 'Do not let any unwholesome talk come out of your mouths, but only what is helpful for building others up according to their needs, that it may benefit those who listen' (Ephesians 4:29).

'It isn't just the substance of what we say (or write or read or hear or see) that concerns me. It's the way we say it,' writes Richard Foster. 'To write pedantically about radiance or infinity or ubiquity stunts the mind and cramps the soul. To find the right word, to capture the perfect image awakens the spirit and enlarges the soul.'

'The word aptly spoken' is the true word, the word of beauty, the word of enrichment. What a different world we would know if everyone did 'speak the truth with his neighbour' (Ephesians 4:25). It would be a world as beautiful as 'apples of gold in settings of silver'.

The liberating Word

'If the Son sets you free, you will be free indeed' (John 8:36).

Philip Yancey believes we may have entered a new Dark Age in which the devil owns the airwaves and when words seem dull compared to the dazzle of virtual reality and CD-ROM. 'I have hope, though,' he writes. 'Despite the waves of hysteria and authoritarianism in church history, words of truth have survived and emerged later as living forces to change individuals and entire cultures.' He believes that in our increasingly oppressive times, we need to remember that 'words have their greatest impact when they enhance freedom, when they liberate.'

Access to a computer, a thesaurus and a graphics programme may conspire to make us lazy in our attempts to communicate the liberating *logos* to a society bound up in the fetters of sin and legalism. In this technological age when affordable publishing tools are at our fingertips and it is suddenly easy to express ourselves with a few key-strokes, we are vulnerable to being washed away in a flood of undocumented, unsubstantiated, off-the-cuff verbiage, which will have little of value to say to the world. Perhaps we will only increase the noise, while the legitimate voices steadily whispering truth are drowned out in the flood's roar.

Conversely, the Spirit-filled communicator will test words in the crucible of life, asking if what we say has nutrition for a world hungry for words that inform, inspire, heal, help. We will meet the price of careful word study, training our ears to catch the cadence of a sentence, the balanced rhythm of a paragraph. We will heed the Scripture's warning that 'we who teach will be judged more strictly' (James 3:1), and we will steep ourselves in reading that inculcates the old universal truths, for without deep study and reflection on what lives for eternity, our words will have no power to liberate.

When Clara Schumann performed musical compositions by her late husband, she always prepared by reading his letters. In so doing, she felt him come alive through her so that she could more accurately and sensitively interpret his great works. As Christians desiring to reflect the truths of our Lord, we will only be able to do so accurately by meditating upon His work and words through the pages of Holy Scripture.

Not only in practice of Scripture study but in all our reading, Eugene Peterson (in his *Take and Read*) calls us to 'spiritual reading', designated *lectio divina* by those in the monastic life. This is reading, not for analytical or entertaining reasons, but for companionship, looking always for Him who inhabits the universe. Peterson says, 'All honest words can involve us in some way, if we read with our hearts as well as our heads, in an eternal conversation that got its start in the Word that "became flesh". "Spiritual reading" is at home with Homer as well as Hosea.'

The Word

By the end of the first century the Christian Church, which had been cradled in Judaism needed to find a way to introduce to non-Jews the values of Christian civilization without these having to be channelled through Judaism. They had to find a way to speak of the great truths of the Christian faith using Greek vocabulary. Since both Jew and Greek possessed the conception of the *logos* of God, John was able to bridge the gap between a transcendent God and the material world. This illustrates what must be the concern of every contemporary Christian – to engage their own culture in language familiar to their friends and neighbours. Because language is always evolving, Christians must recognise the need to speak in the most cogent, colourful language the great truths that hold everlasting life for every person.

In a postmodern world some terms and concepts used by Christians fall outside many people's frame of reference. The lack of common language tends to wall off the Christian world from the secular. Words in common Church parlance such as 'anointing', 'atonement', 'fellowship', 'propitiation', and 'redemption' have become anachronistic. Holiness demands that we give up some of our cherished words in order to penetrate the hearts of modern people who desperately need an understanding of God and His kingdom.

Historian Cyril Barnes tells us that early in his life, William Booth determined to 'read not less than four chapters in God's Word every day'. In 1885 he wrote in *The War Cry* about the Revised Version of the Bible. He considered its publication to be 'the event of the past week'. He complained only that if he had had the arrangements he would have expressed its substance 'not in the stiff and ancient language used 300 years ago but in the form of speech employed by the people of the present day'. He added, 'If the revision throws any new light upon the precious volume – the Book of books – I shall accept it very gratefully. Meanwhile … I want to see a new translation of the Bible into the hearts and conduct of living men and women … It is no use making correct translations of words if we cannot see the words translated into life.'

The last Word

'In the beginning was the Word' (John 1:1). God spoke the universe into being with a word, and light burst upon the threshold of existence with a word. Man was formed of the dust of the earth by the word of the Creator. Nothing is more powerful, nothing more eloquent. 'The grass withers and the flower falls away, but the word of the Lord endures forever' (1 Peter 1: 24-25). May all our words reflect that enduring Word and be to a thirsty world living water that will sustain and satisfy throughout eternity.

CHAPTER 9

OUR MOST PRECIOUS RESOURCE

HOLINESS AND PEOPLE

General Eva Burrows (R)

WHEN I think of Salvationists seeking to re-discover the significance of holiness as part of their daily living as Christians, I am reminded of the story of Isaac in the Old Testament looking for fresh and refreshing water for his people (Genesis 26:18). He decided to 'reopen the wells that had been dug by his father, Abraham' which their enemy, the Philistines, had filled up. So Isaac did not look for new wells. He went to the old wells where he knew he could find water if he cleared them of the debris of the intervening years.

That metaphor has meaning for us as we search the 'old wells' to rediscover this most precious resource of Salvationists who seek to live the holy life in contemporary society. That seeking is not merely from the deep well of Salvation Army history, but more importantly from the source of all sources, that deepest well, the Word of God. The Bible is both our source and resource. Its root teaching is of the holy God of the Old Testament, of the character and life of Jesus Christ in the New Testament and in the significance of the Holy Spirit as God's empowering presence enabling us to respond to God's call to holy living.

Holiness is attainable

To Salvationists, holiness is a spiritual ideal, but many are not really convinced that it is an attainable experience. I think this problem arises because we so often speak about holiness in terms of behaviour and morality, in terms of restrictions and prohibitions, as though it were some kind of code of spiritual etiquette, or a list of things you *do not* do.

However, holiness is a much more positive, practical and wholesome experience than that. It is a quality of character to which God calls his people, and if He calls us to it, it must be possible. It involves the whole of my life, my relationship with the people I rub shoulders with every day, the plans I make for my future, the way I spend my recreation, and the time I give to my church responsibilities. Holiness is not so much about what I give up, as about what I take on.

Holiness is not a theologically abstract concept, but as General John Larsson writes:

Holiness ought not to be so much the pursuit of a particular religious experience, as a day to day, indeed moment by moment, experience of seeking to live by the grace of God an ever more Christ-like life in a sinful world.

The emphasis on growth in Christlikeness is seen in the writings of our 'apostle of holiness', Samuel Logan Brengle, who spoke of 'becoming more and more like Jesus'. This understanding is taken further by one of our more modern apostles of holiness, Frederick Coutts. I once heard General Coutts give a most succinct definition of holiness in a mere thirteen words:

Holiness is a relationship with God that increasingly expresses itself in Christ-like living.

This definition appeals to me because it calls holiness 'a relationship'; we are not reaching after holiness, but reaching after God in a relationship that needs to be cultivated. So first of all we have to look at the reality and depth of our relationship with God. I like the word 'increasingly' because it indicates that holiness is not a static experience. Once we've got holiness, that's it? No! It is a growing, developing, increasingly real experience. I like the word 'Christ-like'. Holiness is seen in reality in the ideal life of Jesus Christ, and through our relationship with God we are being conformed to Christ's likeness, as His qualities and attributes are being developed and seen in our character and conduct.

I especially like this definition because it is Scriptural. As the Apostle Paul writes to the Corinthian Christians:

And we, who with unveiled faces all reflect the Lord's glory, are being transformed into his likeness with ever-increasing glory, which comes from the Lord who is the Spirit (2 Corinthians 3: 18).

So holiness is truly an attainable experience for every believer through the work of God the Holy Spirit in our lives. It is the will of God. Paul writes that God has chosen us so that 'we should be conformed to the likeness of his Son' (Romans 8: 29).

Army doctrine

Our Doctrine books give the same guidance. The 1969 edition states:

Holiness in man is the moral quality of character and conduct by those who, through the indwelling Spirit, share Christ's nature and consent to be ruled by him.

In the 1998 edition, *Salvation Story*, we find:

To see Christ is to understand the nature of holiness, and to follow him is to be marked by it. Holiness is Christlikeness ... the realisation of the Christ-life within us.

No wonder the desire for holiness, for Christlikeness, is a desire, a longing in the heart of all Christians, and an indication of spiritual health. Dr J.I. Packer in his profound, yet clear, teaching on holiness writes:

God has implanted a passion for holiness deep in every born-again heart. Holiness, which means being near God, like God, given to God and pleasing God, is something believers want more than anything else in the world ... It is normal and natural for Christians to want to understand and prove the Spirit's sanctifying power.

Two dimensions of holiness

Holiness has both vertical and horizontal dimensions. It is not just a private matter between me and God, or confined to individual piety. God's concern for holy living is not limited to personal spiritual awakenings within me. His intention is to send me out into the world to live a powerful, influential Christ-like life. My Salvation Army corps officer (pastor), speaking on 'Holiness Now', began his message with this significant sentence: 'Holiness is about being people of integrity and compassion.' He went on to say: 'There must be worship within the holy place, then there will be outward service to glorify God.' He was helping us grasp the two dimensional nature of the holy life.

The prophet Isaiah caught this same perspective when he had an awesome personal experience of the holy God in the sacred atmosphere of the temple in Jerusalem. After the awareness of personal cleansing (first dimension), God sent him out into the world of people and problems (second dimension). Isaiah, filled with a new God-life, was eager and ready to go and live it out.

The contemporary meaning of that experience for us is that holiness must be lived out in the traffic of everyday life: on the factory floor, in the office and the boardroom, in the college classroom, in the home, in the community and to a needy, and often godless world.

Dr Donald E. Burke, of the Army's William and Catherine Booth Bible College in Winnipeg, writes:

Holiness is inherently social in nature. Personal holiness cannot rest isolated from the world. Rather it seeks to embrace the world in the name of a holy God.

Jesus, the Holy One, embodied that, and prayed in the upper room for his disciples and for us: 'Father, I pray that you will not take them out of the world, but keep them from the evil in the world.' He is still making that prayer, as He intercedes for us at the right hand of God the Father. Our pattern, our role model is Christ Jesus Himself. He never talked much about holiness, but He lived it. His life spoke for itself. Holiness became flesh and dwelt among us. Jesus was holiness made visible.

He was involved with the world of 'people, people, people', always concerned for those who milled about Him, never self-absorbed. He made friends with people of unsavoury character and lifestyle, yet He lived an unblemished life. He had a powerful impact on all He met.

People wanted to be near Him, aware of his spiritual power. He had meaningful relationships with people, bringing them alive with his truth in conversation, aware of their needs.

Evelyn Underhill reminds us:

No amount of words can explain holiness, but an encounter with it amazes and delights, shames and convinces us all at once.

When I encounter Jesus in the Gospels that happens to me and I long to be like Him.

People relationships

The Lord's shining goodness was seen always in His relationships with people and that is where holiness is seen at its most attractive and most convincing. Life is made up of relationships. We function really well as human beings only when we function well in relation to others – our family, our friends, our neighbours, our workmates, the people in the corps or congregation, and in the community. These are the people we mix with every day, the people of our life. I think I am right when I say that most of our problems arise from our inability to relate effectively to others.

It was the French existentialist philosopher, Dr. Jean-Paul Sartre, who once wrote: 'Hell is other people.' Now Dr. Sartre may have been a brilliant man, but that statement is foolish and intemperate. Other people may complicate our lives and give us untold anxieties, but without them life would be desolate and superficial. Hell is when you think only of yourself, selfishly using other people to your own advantage, and seeing people only in terms of what they can do for you, thereby corroding all your relationships and ending up in a lonely hell of your own making.

Indeed, it is in the context of relating to others that we best work out our life. It is in this context that we reveal the meaning of holiness. The holy life is a life of love. Jesus not only lived it, but He taught it. He told us to love others as He has loved us (John 13:34). Living the holy life means nothing unless we reach out to love the neighbour whom we know, the stranger in our midst, the loveless, the hopeless and the hurting.

Someone has said that we can relate to others in three ways:

- we move away from others behind protective barriers, fearing close relationships, living in isolation;
- we move against others in conflict situations, pulling against each other in a clash of personalities;
- we move towards others, on the lookout for ways to help and support them.

Only this third way is the Christ-like way, treating others as Christ treats us, seeking to be patient with others as Christ is patient with us.

Love for people

The love of Jesus can be 'shed abroad in our hearts' by the Holy Spirit, and we are enabled to love others as he loved us. What astonishing, forgiving, unselfish love Jesus showed to us. The fruits of the indwelling Holy Spirit in our lives are really a list of the qualities of Christ's own character, and the first of that wonderful list of nine is *love*. Indeed, most of the nine fruits, indicators of holy living, concern our relationship with others – love, joy peace, patience, kindness, goodness, faithfulness, gentleness, self-control. Now *that* is a holy life-style. When those qualities identify Christians, by the grace of Jesus and through the power of the Holy Spirit, they will unconsciously live out the life of holiness. People who encounter them will recognise it and be amazed and delighted all at once.

One such Spirit-filled Christian was the late Brigadier Josef Korbel, the writer of *In My Enemy's Camp*. I heard him tell of his days of imprisonment in the communist labour camp in Czechoslovakia. He and other prisoners were near to starvation, but issued with only one piece of bread each day. When other prisoners hungrily bolted down their bread, Korbel divided his into three pieces. One he ate slowly and the other two he kept in his pocket. Later in the day as he ate his second piece, a fellow prisoner would eye him jealously and say, 'Where did you get extra bread?' Korbel would reply: 'Nowhere. I have kept some of my own back. Have a share of mine.' Then he would give his last piece to the ravenous man. It is no wonder that his selfless love made such an impression on others, and why so many of his fellow prisoners came to accept the Christ whom Korbel loved and served.

God sanctifies us in order to mark our character with the Spirit of Jesus, and then He wants us to take that same character out and mark the world with the Spirit of Jesus. True holiness engenders a compassion that will naturally reach out in ministry, mission and service of one kind or another.

John Wesley, whose teaching on holiness is a basic ingredient of The Salvation Army's teaching, lived out his belief that involvement with people was an indispensable component of holy living. He wrote: 'There is no holiness but social holiness.' That can take many expressions – not only 'loving your neighbour', but speaking out on policies that fail to protect fellow citizens, denouncing social injustice as did the holy prophets of old, or offering compassionate service to the needy and destitute in the name of Jesus Christ.

Holiness as a hallmark

'Holiness unto the Lord' is as much a Salvation Army motto as 'Blood and Fire'. Those biblical words, 'Holiness unto the Lord', were engraved on the badge worn on a priest's forehead as he served in the holy temple. However, the prophet Zechariah showed that holiness is not limited to the sacred place, for he saw in a vision 'Holiness unto the Lord' inscribed 'on the harness bells of horses' in the traffic of life. Also he saw the words inscribed on 'all the cooking pots in the kitchens in Jerusalem and Judah' (Zechariah 14: 20, 21, *The Message*).

God wants to see holiness identifying our lives in the home as well as out in the community, in family relationships, in our attitudes and actions towards one another, and in marriages. I read once that Mrs Commissioner Brengle had the words 'Holiness unto the Lord' engraved on the inside of her wedding ring. Perhaps the home may be the hardest place to live out holiness. It is a place where our imperfections, our faults, our failings are well known. However, the home should be the place where the Spirit of Jesus, the loving Holy Spirit, permeates our lives, and directs our behaviour.

'Holiness and People' are inextricably bound together. It is about giving oneself totally to Christ, and giving oneself willingly to others. Let 'Holiness unto the Lord' and holy relationships with other people be the hallmarks of our lives and our most precious resource. May we seek to embrace all peoples of the world in the name of a holy God.

CHAPTER 10

WHERE HAVE WE COME FROM?

HOLINESS AND OUR HERITAGE

Colonel Henry Gariepy

WHEN we come to God, He accepts us just as we are, but He does not leave us there. The Lord does not leave us where He found us. Our spiritual need is not only for atonement, but also for attunement. Through the atoning work of Christ we are adopted into the family of God. Through the cleansing work of the Spirit we are adapted into the family of God.

Salvationists firmly believe, on the authority of the Word of God and validated by experience, that besides salvation there is sanctification; besides forgiveness of sins there is deliverance from sin; besides being 'born of the Spirit' there is being 'filled with the Spirit'. God calls us to holiness, to power and purity, that His marred image may again be restored in us.

Pathfinders of the Army's position

John Wesley (1703-1791) is regarded as the father of the modern holiness movement. The providential legacy of his preaching and teaching ministry spawned the Methodist churches and their offshoots. Beginning with John Wesley there came nothing less than a rediscovery of New Testament doctrine concerning holiness. As the chief architect of the doctrine of entire sanctification, Wesley's teaching has become a cornerstone of the Army's position on holiness. A *Plain Account of Christian Perfection* records his own experience of discovering this truth.

The holiness movement and its doctrine could not be confined within Wesleyan boundaries; it was too big to be denominational. Others, who followed in the wake of the Methodist pathfinder, explored anew its exegetical aspects and experiential practicalities. From the roots of Wesleyanism there sprang up vigorous and fruitful branches, including The Salvation Army founded by William and Catherine Booth. The Booths were influenced by the holiness teachings of both John and Charles Wesley, Phoebe Palmer, George Fox and the Quakers, Charles Finney, and other exponents of the deeper life.

The Booths and their followers proclaimed a twofold salvation – 'Blood and Fire' – the forgiveness of sin by the cleansing power of the

Saviour's blood, and full salvation by the cleansing power of the Spirit's sanctifying work. Holiness became staple theology in the early days of the Army, enshrined as its tenth of eleven doctrines. Samuel Logan Brengle became the Army's 'Apostle of Holiness', his series of books on the topic having a wide readership both within the Army as well as among holiness movements outside the Army.

Where the Army stands

Holiness, like many intangibles, does not lend itself to easy definition. Some might define it negatively as absence of sin, or positively as absolute virtue or moral perfection. Yet all such definitions remain abstract.

We could also define holiness by its ramifications, acknowledging that it is theologically valid, theoretically reasonable, philosophically our highest good, psychologically sound, ethically imperative, sociologically essential, biblically commanded, and experientially a glorious possibility. These grandiose descriptions though true, fall short of the most essential definition of holiness.

In reviewing John Wesley's heritage of holiness teaching, we cannot avoid the term he used, 'Christian perfection'. Wesley's terms at time caused even him discomfort. In a letter to his brother Charles (Works, vol. 12) he wrote, 'I am at my wit's end with regard to Christian perfection. Shall we go on asserting perfection against all the world? Or shall we quietly let it drop?' However insistently John Wesley may have preached and urged 'Christian perfection' or entire sanctification, he never once claimed it; rather he disclaimed it. In a letter to Dr. William Dodd, he wrote, 'I tell you flat, I have not attained the character I draw.'

Various terms have sought to describe the experience of holiness. Besides Wesley's terms, 'Christian perfection' and 'perfect love', it has been called 'heart purity', 'filled with the Spirit', 'full salvation', 'second blessing', and 'the blessing of a clean heart'. Holiness is a multi-faceted jewel of the Christian life, and each term shows but one facet of its blessing.

As with all doctrines, it has bred its controversies under such banners as 'eradicationists', 'suppressionists', 'counteractionists', and so on. A gentle hint: it is better to be a consumer of its truth than to be a connoisseur of its terms.

Usually, though not of unvarying necessity, sanctification is perceived by many as a post-conversion crisis. The believer, although rejoicing in sins forgiven, becomes concerned, even dismayed, by inward defeat, unholy thoughts and desires, superficial spirituality, and unreality in prayer. These are coupled with a deep longing to know complete victory over sin, a closer fellowship with Christ, and a purity of heart. Thus the heart set on sanctification reaches a crisis-point, culminating with full surrender, an inward renewal and a glad spontaneity to live a Christ-like life.

In the Greek New Testament, the root *hag* is the basis of *hagiasmos*, translated 'holiness', 'consecration', 'sanctification'. The *hag* words, like Hebrew's *qadosh*, literally mean 'separate, contrasting with the profane'. Certain times were holy in that they were set apart: the Sabbath (Genesis 2:3) and festivals (Leviticus 23: 4-44). Certain places were holy: Jerusalem (Isaiah 11:9), the Tabernacle (Exodus 25), the Temple (Ezekiel 40-48) and all related objects. The priests and Levites were separated unto God and as such were holy. Thus 'separation' is a major concept and a dynamic dimension of holiness. When God calls us to be holy, He calls us to be separate from the unclean things of the world, and separated unto Himself. Thus The Salvation Army's 'Soldier's Covenant' invokes a holy separation, including our vow of total abstinence from 'all that could enslave the body or spirit'.

A pressing of 'separation' beyond reason has resulted in some people becoming monks and hermits. Possibly the pinnacle (!) of this lifestyle was achieved when Simeon Stylites, a monk who died in A.D. 459, remained for 35 years on a small platform on top of a 50-foot stone pillar in Syria, in order to be 'separate from the world'. For this feat, his church made him a saint!

We remember the petition of our Lord for His disciples, 'I pray not that you should take them out of the world, but that you should keep them from evil' (John 17:15). In other words, although we are in the world – the world must not be in us.

Let no one imagine that holiness is a state of grace in which we are utterly free from all the wiles of Satan. Any who has based his hope on that kind of experience will have it shattered and be disillusioned. We are engaged in fierce spiritual combat, with no demilitarised zone for the Christian.

More than we need holiness described, we need to see it revealed. One who came to us clothed in our humanity, declared, 'He that has seen Me has seen the Father.' In Christ, holiness comes alive, not merely as a definition, but as a visible incarnation. There can be no better definition for holiness than 'Holiness is Christlikeness'. In Christ we see all the fruit of the Spirit come to perfect fulfilment in our humanity. Jesus Christ is our highest definition and declaration of holiness.

Salvationists believe that the holiness taught in the New Testament, and exemplified in the life of Christ, is that state where the devil is defeated and sin is shunned, where our will is in harmony with the will of God, where the Holy Spirit rules the life in motive, affection, and action, where we may be beset by temptations but have the mastery over them. Sanctification is God at work in our lives: shaping our characters, purifying our hearts, tutoring our minds, strengthening our wills, and actualising our highest spiritual potential. Holiness is not so much an experience to be sought for its own sake, but rather is a by-product of a life fully consecrated to Christ.

The Army's biblical mandate

Our doctrine of holiness is derived, not from our doctrine book, not from John Wesley, not from Samuel Brengle, but from the very heart of Scripture. Holiness is highly important to God, with the word 'holiness' found no less than 650 times in the Bible. The first call to holiness is sounded in the ancient book of Leviticus. The theme and keyword in Leviticus is holiness, occurring more than 80 times. Historically and typologically, Leviticus sets forth the fatal character of sin, God's provision of an atoning sacrifice, and his command to holiness. A detailed interpretation of Leviticus is given in the Book of Hebrews, its rituals and types having ultimate fulfilment in Christ.

Way back in Leviticus, over the vestibule of Israel's theocracy, there sounded the first and supreme requirement: 'You shall be holy; for I the Lord your God am holy' (Leviticus 11:44, 45; 19:2; 20:7). God's call to holiness was not something new that came late in the history of mankind, but from the very beginning was His will for all people. God's call to holiness in this ancient book gives the foundation for holiness. It is the very nature of God – 'because I am holy'. In the Bible the attribute of God's holiness is stressed more than any other. It is the only attribute thrice repeated: 'Holy, holy, holy is the Lord Almighty' (Isaiah 6:3; Revelation 4:8). God wants us to be holy so that we as His children will be like Him, restored to His image, pure and undefiled. Of course, that which is absolute can be only relative, when reflected in us.

The Psalms resonate with God's call to holiness. 'Worship the Lord in the splendour of his holiness' is God's call through his poet psalmist (29:2; 96:9). 'Splendour' is defined as 'dazzling brightness, grandeur', and is compatibly yoked together with 'holiness' in this text. This verse has been set to a contemporary devotional tune for praise and worship, reminding us three millennia later of God's gracious invitation and requisite for worship.

Prophets picked up the theme of holiness. In the Book of Zechariah no less than 15 verses in the final three chapters begin with the words, 'on that day'. They refer to the end times, the day to which all history inexorably moves. On that day when the Lord will return in mighty triumph, 'Holy to the Lord' will be the inscription throughout the eternal kingdom (14: 20-21). God is a holy God, who calls for a holy people, to dwell with Him forever in His holy kingdom.

We turn to the pages of the New Testament and in Peter's epistle we hear the echo of God's call in Leviticus: 'But just as he who called you is holy, so be holy in all you do; for it is written: "Be holy, because I am holy"' (1 Peter 1: 15-16). This epistle was written as a manual of survival for Christians under siege, to a church suffering violent persecution.

In times of trial and testing, holiness of heart and life will bring the needed strength and adequacy.

The Apostle Paul reminds believers that the fruit of our salvation leads to a holy life: 'But now that you have been set free from sin and have become slaves to God, the benefit you reap leads to holiness, and the result is eternal life' (Romans 6:22). He further writes in 1 Thessalonians 4:3, 'It is God's will that you should be holy.'

As we put our ear up close to the door of the upper room where our Lord met for the final time with His disciples, we come upon one of the most sacred and sublime discourses of the Master. That intimate and sacred fellowship culminates with His high priestly prayer, for His disciples and for His followers of all ages. What is it that He implores his heavenly Father to do for them, and for us? 'Sanctify them' is His prayer in those final hours of his earthly life and ministry (John 17:17). As the old spiritual reminds us, 'That was my Lord, He was praying for me.'

Indeed, the holiness teaching of The Salvation Army rests upon the solid foundation of the Word of God. Even its credal statement of holiness doctrine echoes the text of 1 Thessalonians 5:23.

The challenge of history

History reveals that the original vision and vigour of spiritual movements scarcely outlive two or three generations. If that is so, let us beware; we Salvationists may be living on borrowed time. Luther's reformation in Germany became Hitler's ruthless Germany. Africa, once a stronghold of early Christianity, is now a seat of Islam. Europe and England, once the seedbed of missions, are now plagued by spiritual barrenness. Trends of godlessness today threaten the moral foundations upon which America was founded.

What is true of nations is sadly true of denominations. News headlines expose the slippery slope of accommodation to today's relativisation of values by once thriving churches and denominations. An instructive insight from the history of the Christian Church reveals that when it suffered the most, it prospered the most. It became axiomatic that 'the blood of the martyrs became the seed of the Christian church.' Read again the colourful and inspiring history of our own movement, of its persecution, its heroes, its call by God to serve out there where the air was blowing, where the issues were real, where people were hurting. The Salvation Army was born to battle, cradled in the trenches of spiritual warfare, called to be the Lord's infantry of the militant Christian church. Those were the days of our most rapid growth.

The Christian church must always beware of the perils of prosperity. Let not our epitaph be 'We can handle adversity, but our prosperity is killing us.' The church that marries the spirit of an age becomes a widow in the next generation. Let us steer by the stars, and not by the light of each passing ship.

We look at our current literature and ask, 'Where today are the holiness writings that once graced our publications?' We look to our platforms and ask, 'Who have come to stand in the place of the great hearts whose crystal clear teachings on sanctification linger with us? Where are the successors to such holiness exponents as Catherine Booth, Samuel Brengle, Albert Pepper, Allister Smith, Frederick Coutts, Edward Read?' Catherine Booth is said to have lamented on her deathbed, 'Oh Kate, why can't God keep a movement pure for more than one generation?' Indeed, vigilance must keep our movement spiritually alive, though God buries his workmen.

The Army and holiness today

Holiness is in the DNA of The Salvation Army; God has put it in our spiritual genes. Today there are vital and virile efforts within our beloved Army to nurture its ongoing teaching and standard of Salvationist lifestyle. A priority on the curriculum of every Salvation Army School/ College for Officer Training is the Bible's teaching on holiness. No Salvation Army officer is commissioned and ordained without having been exposed to the Army's doctrine on holiness, and called to incorporate its teaching into their life and ministry.

Brengle Memorial Holiness Institutes, now held around the Army world, offer curricula for soldiers and officers on the subject of holiness. *A Salvationist Treasury*, released in 2000 by the Army's Crest Books label in the USA, brought to its readers a compendium of both classic and contemporary writings on holiness. During a visit of officer cadets to our corps, a woman cadet preached on the subject of holiness. Though not presented with polished oratory, the preachment elicited hearty 'amens' from veteran Salvationists that morning in the congregation. It was a sign that we wish to be true to our birthright and that within the Army our tenth doctrine is alive and well. It declares: 'We believe that it is the privilege of all believers to be wholly sanctified, and that their whole spirit and soul and body may be preserved blameless unto the coming of our Lord Jesus Christ.'

Our Salvation Army Song Book presents a treasure trove of hymns that call us to holiness and give voice to our heart's inarticulate longings. Both holiness doctrine and experience are enshrined in the bounty of devotional offerings by Charles Wesley, along with Salvationists Albert Orsborn, John Lawley, Herbert Booth, William Pearson, Ruth Tracy, Catherine Baird, Brindley Boon and a host of other inspired lyricists. These holiness songs ring true both theologically and experientially, and continue to give impetus to keep alive the Army's rich heritage of holiness.

During a conference of Christian workers convened by D.L. Moody, various addresses were given on how Christians could live a holier, more useful life. At the conclusion of the two-hour session, Mr Moody, who was acting as chairman, rose and said, 'I can tell you in five words how Christians can become more holy and useful – be filled with the Spirit!' Salvationists believe that the secret of a holy life is just that, being filled with the Spirit. The word 'fire', emblazoned on our tricolour, symbolises for Salvationists the cleansing work of the Spirit.

Christianity's belief in the Person and work of Holy Spirit is unique among world religions. Buddhism, Islam, etc. pay homage to a god or gods, but the gods remain 'out there' at a safe distance. They do not come and reside within believers in an intimate way. This is a unique and dynamic note of our Christian faith. The audacious Christian view of God is that the third Person in the Godhead, the Holy Spirit, actually resides within us, accomplishing our spiritual cleansing and empowering.

We are the beneficiaries of each member, or Person, of the Trinity. God the Father is God above us; God the Son is God for us; God the Holy Spirit is God in us. God the Father is for us the divine Intention, God the Son the divine Invasion, and God the Spirit the divine Indwelling. God the Father purposed our salvation; God the Son provided our salvation, and God the Holy Spirit perfects our salvation.

In the heart of the epistle to the Romans, the Apostle Paul shares his moving spiritual autobiography. He writes of the duality in his spiritual nature – a civil war within his soul in his struggle between the carnal and spiritual natures (7: 15-23). The J.B. Phillips translation renders Paul's melancholy frustration and failure in verse 15: 'My own behaviour baffles me. For I find myself not doing what I really want to do but doing what I really loathe.' He cries out in despair, 'Who will rescue me from this body of death?' (7: 24).

God does not leave us there, struggling with the desires and depravity of our fallen nature, with an irreconcilable conflict between the flesh and the spirit, with an unfilled longing for deliverance from indwelling sin. With assurance, Paul says, 'I thank God through Jesus Christ our Lord.' He goes on in the next chapter, often called 'the Holy Spirit chapter' of the Bible, to bring us to the high altar of holiness. Here Paul progresses from under the tyranny of his carnal nature, into a new and radical relationship of life in Christ, that of liberty through the life in the Spirit (8: 1-4). The crowning point of New Testament revelation on holiness is reached in its doctrine of the Holy Spirit. That holiness which is likeness to God, and is exhibited in Christ, is brought about by the Holy Spirit within the fully indwelt Christian believer.

Jesus' promise of the gift of the Holy Spirit is the great heritage of every child of God, the very gift of God himself, living within us, creating within us the beautiful 'fruit of the Spirit' (Galatians 5: 22-23). Salvationists hold that the heights of holiness are within reach of every believer. This cannot be achieved; it must be received. This is not a state that we attain by self-effort; it is an inwrought renovation that we obtain by the Holy Spirit. The precondition for holiness is to be completely yielded to Christ, and to being indwelt by the Holy Spirit.

Holiness still relevant

It has been suggested that the word 'holiness' has lost its sheen, its attractiveness, caked with mould and shrouded with funeral flowers. However, God never uses an eraser or a 'delete' key in what He has written in his Word to us. 'Holiness' will always be one of the most sacred words in the Bible, because it defines the nature of God, and it is the highest privilege of the believer. The words that adorn the holiness tables in our Salvation Army halls and worship chapels, derived from the Word of God, 'Holiness unto the Lord', serve still as an apt motto and mandate for Salvationists.

Some years ago, with friends, I took on the challenge and exhilarating experience of hiking up one of the highest mountains in the Colorado Rockies. As we made our ascent, we came to the timberline where nothing grows above that point and with only forbidding rocks and the heights beyond. Ahead of us there loomed a high summit etched against an azure sky, but when we finally reached that point, we found yet another summit beyond, and to our surprise still higher peaks beyond each visible summit, each opening more vast and beautiful vistas of scenery below.

That mountain experience can be a parable of our spiritual journey. Of course its final summit will not be reached in this life, but as we continue to make our ascent to the heights to which God calls us, we are enabled to go from 'strength to strength', from 'peak to peak', from 'height to height'. Isaiah described it long ago in his memorable metaphor: 'And a highway will be there; it will be called the Way of Holiness' (35:8). Holiness is not a state or a status, but a lifetime walk.

With the songwriter we pray, 'A higher plane than I have found, Lord, plant my feet on higher ground.' Let us be excited about the further summits and exhilarating vistas God has in store for us as we make our pilgrimage on the Highway of Holiness.

CHAPTER 11

PROVEN TRUSTWORTHY?

HOLINESS AND THE MAKING OF COVENANTS

Captain Stephen Court

Covenant always involves death

YOU can't cut a covenant without bloodshed. In fact, that is what the cutting is all about. Whether it is Abraham and God, a Junior Soldier enrolment on a Sunday morning, or Jesus on the Cross, covenant always involves death. Maybe that is why it is not a popular thing. Who wants to die? Who wants to die to self, to comfort, to habits, to ease? Who wants to suffer? For that reason, the binding agreement of covenant, used spiritually (it can be used socially and commercially too), has been a heavily under-rated aspect of Christianity throughout the centuries.

It is having an even tougher time in millennium three. Some apologetic Army officers and soldiers, burdened by a spiritual inferiority complex, figure that we cannot challenge anyone to sign her life away in covenant with God through the Army. This attitude completely misses the mystery and power of covenant. If we were living it, we wouldn't even have to raise the issue. Unapologetic, romantic, heroic warfare remains as attractive and captivating today as it was 130 years ago with the Army's first salvos, or 2,000 years ago with the 33 AD Calvary salvos. The crazy thing is, when we're living in holy covenant, it is not a garment that we put on; it is rather a passion that bursts out of us.

However, that might sound like drivel to the uninformed and uninitiated. Where is that romantic heroic warfare? Where are the signs and wonders that George Scott Railton celebrated? (That great Army saint said, 'What is to be won for God must be captured from the devil. Not indeed, by human might or power, but by the use of all men's powers under the mighty influence of the Holy Spirit are signs and wonders continually possible.') Where too are the supernatural gifts that William Booth cherished? Where is God's delight?

God's delight

What we have lost, we have lost through the loss of covenant. Our Father 'delights' to give us the Kingdom (Luke 12:32, Young's Literal

Translation). As well as peace, righteousness, and joy in the Holy Spirit (Romans 14:17, NBV), the Kingdom involves all sorts of supernatural interventions. Our Father would love to delight in us by releasing the fullness of His Kingdom, if He could trust us with it. 'We cannot earn God's love, but we can earn His trust,' a friend wrote to me. Like Elisha, after picking up the mantle, our covenant provides a holy trustworthiness that allows God to release Kingdom fullness and, in so doing, take delight in us. Do we want the wonder-working, world-winning power of the Kingdom that God delights to give us? One of the keys is the trust generated only by covenant holiness. We look now at the power of covenant.

The Nazirites

You may remember the Nazirites. Described in Numbers 6, the Nazirites, which means 'separated', took a special covenanted vow before God. Covenant sets people apart. This is an important definition of holiness in the Old Testament. These people were characterised by their holiness, their submitted, sacrificial obedience. Now, there were some inconvenient conditions to the Nazirite vow. You couldn't cut your hair, you couldn't touch dead bodies, you couldn't drink wine – that sort of thing. It doesn't sound like the most popular way of life, but it seems to have been pretty effective. We know only a few Nazirites in the Bible, and all of them were wonder-working world-winners:

- Samson (Judges 13ff) demonstrated superhuman power in leading Israel in revolt against the Philistines. Among other things, he killed one thousand enemy troops with the jawbone of a donkey.

- Samuel (1 Samuel 1: 11, 28) led Israel into its golden era, and all the while none of his words fell to the ground (that is, he was a very accurate prophet). He dragged a rag-tag collection of tribes into nationhood.

- John the Baptist (Luke 1:15) lived a fasted, prophetic lifestyle that ushered in the way of the Lord. He survived by eating the predatory locust insects – he destroyed the destroyer.

- Paul (Acts 21: 23-26) performed all kinds of miracles while spreading the Gospel around the known world. Paul took Truth from a hidden corner of an empire and pioneered the largest religion in the world.

Not a bad line-up, eh? I mean, imagine going out to do evangelism with those four! Or even with one at a time, or in pairs? Samuel would download hidden details of some person's life that could open them up to the Gospel. Samson would give the General's elbow to any wayward Hell's Angels. John would put the fear of God into anyone with a religious spirit. You could tag along with Paul while he kicked demons and healed sick people!

Each of these Nazirites was, by definition, in covenant relationship with God. Their power came from the covenant. The only breach of the Nazirite covenant recorded in Scripture, the notorious episode of Samson's haircut, actually exposes a *spiritual* breach of covenant. Samson, dogged to frustration by the persistence of Delilah, finally capitulated. 'Wearied to death,' Samson, 'opened to her his whole heart' (Judges 16: 16,17, NBV). Of course, his heart belonged only to God. So he accompanied physical adultery with spiritual adultery. Samson's wonder-working, world-winning power came out of covenant with God. His loss of power came out of breach of covenant with God. When he compromised his intimate loyalty to God, forfeiting his holy covenant, he gave up his power. It was only as he renewed covenant, and as his hair began to grow again in covenant obedience, that his power returned.

God is a covenant-keeping God. He is all about covenant. If we don't understand covenant, we don't understand God. Throughout history God has used covenant to 'bind' Himself to us in solemn agreement. Here are a few key examples:

- Genesis 9: 9-17 (with Noah and a rainbow);
- Genesis 15: 18 (with Abraham and descendants);
- Exodus 19:5; 24:7-8; 34:10, 27-28 (with Israel at Sinai);
- 2 Samuel 7; 1 Chronicles 17; Psalm 89:3,28,34,39; 129:12 (with David for an everlasting kingdom).

Covenant is part of what characterises God. It is a key manifestation of His holiness. It is therefore meant to characterise us. It provides for the manifestation of our holiness.

The Rechabites

The Rechabites were an undistinguished clan notable for only one thing – covenant (Jeremiah 35:6,7). The Rechabites grabbed hold of a simple instruction and lived by it faithfully. During a particularly inglorious period in Israel's history, Jeremiah received from the Lord a prophetic word based on the Rechabite covenant people. Their lives were used as a testimony against the behaviour of the Israelites.

It wasn't pleasant to be a covenant people like the Rechabites. They sacrificed many things to keep their covenant. They could not enjoy wine and so were consistently out of place during social gatherings. They could never put down roots and so were always having to adjust, to meet new people, to establish credibility in commercial relationships, to start over again. They could never build houses and so lacked a sense of belonging, at least in a physical sense. Yet God provided. God called them, 'the house of Rechabites' (Jeremiah 35:2, NBV). Ironically, though they lacked a physical building, they possessed the spiritual reality (it sounds a bit like a Salvationist people who have no sacraments but possess the spiritual reality behind them). Not only that, but their 'house' was a travelling tent. This was the sign of their covenant. They were known for their covenant (does it sound familiar, almost like a uniform?).

As well as rejecting wine, the Rechabites were a mobile people, free to follow God wherever He led. They were an example to the people of God. This is a great legacy, but that is not all. Their most famous son was a man named Johonadab. His fleeting career in Scripture graphically depicts the passion and impact of a covenant warrior. Johonadab shows up briefly in 2 Kings 10:15. The Israelite Kingdom had split, and a series of counterfeits reigned in the Northern Kingdom. God, through Elisha, anointed the zealous warrior Jehu to rain down judgement on the disobedient people. Jehu, driving 'like a madman' (2 Kings 9:20, NBV), chased down the Kings of Judah and Israel, killing them both. He then killed Jezebel, the queen mother. Though King Joram was dead, there were 70 other sons of Ahab, all in line for the throne. So Jehu wrote to their guardians, challenging them to fight for the throne. Too afraid to face this warrior, they asked for peace. The terms for peace were the heads of all 70 heirs in two piles by the city gate!

In this moment of national turmoil Jehu turned to the Rechabite, Johonadab, for help. Merciless in their hatred of sin, and complete in their obedience to the commands of God, the two of them killed off the rest of the extended family of King Ahab in Samaria, but they weren't finished. They called a massive solemn assembly for the god Baal, commanding the attendance of every Baal worshipper in the country. The catch was this, if you didn't show, you'd be killed. Understandably, they all showed up. Jehu and Johonadab made sure there were no true Yahweh worshippers present. Then the pagan worship began. While the sacrifices were being offered, Jehu ordered his soldiers to move in and kill every Baal worshipper. They then demolished the pagan temple.

Johonadab, the covenant-keeper, offered credibility to the revolutionary would-be king. He imparted stability during this chaotic political transition. His covenant integrity was an implicit endorsement of Jehu. When added to the traditional characteristics of the Rechabites – fidelity, loyalty, mobility – this combination of integrity with an absolute intolerance of sin makes for a very dangerous front against the enemy.

Now, Johonadab couldn't be mistaken for a wonder-working world-winner, but he *was* in covenant. Such a holy warrior is a formidable opponent for the devil who would much rather feed on carnal Christians.

He'd much rather keep you out of the race. He'd much rather flatter you with comfort, flummox you with commercialism, and fool you with the world's last remaining so called 'virtue', tolerance.

For the Nazirite, covenant brought purity and power. For the Rechabite, covenant provided fidelity, loyalty, mobility, integrity, and a jealousy for the holiness of God. What then does covenant reveal in Salvationists?

The Salvationists

Before answering this question, we have to affirm that the Salvationist has more in common with the Nazirites and the Rechabites than with Baptists or Presbyterians. Did you hear that? We generally line ourselves up alongside the conservative evangelical Protestant churches. True, we hold to Protestant doctrines. Historically, Protestants testified to Biblical truth in the face of the excesses and heresies of the Roman Church in the 16th century. ('Protestant' comes from the Latin, *protestari*, meaning, 'to witness' or 'to testify'. It does not mean 'to protest'.) We are not in direct historical descent from Protestantism, but we are Protestant doctrinally. We flow out of the holiness stream of John Wesley, originally an Anglican priest. What distinguishes us today? Not bands, not songsters, not Home League, etc. What distinguishes us is covenant. We are the most covenanted people I know.

The most covenanted people I know

How many in The Salvation Army would identify covenant as the most important distinctive? General Booth argued that covenant is essential, 'not only for those who do wrong, but to prevent people from going wrong' (William Booth, 'Staff Council Notes', quoted in *The Officer*, March, 2003).

We've watered down our end of the covenant so much that soldiership, for some, has come to mean just signing a piece of paper (and perhaps going to a Saturday seminar so that you can join the band!).

However, the 'Articles of War' and the 'Soldier's Covenant' are intended to provide a means to holiness. The Junior Soldier's Promise (Covenant) and the Officer's Covenant have the same purpose. This puts reins on good intentions to accomplish great ends.

The stakes are so high. Listen to Catherine Booth, writing in 1892:

> *Let me remind you – and it makes my own soul almost reel to think of it – that God holds us responsible. He holds you responsible for all the good you might do if you had (the power of the Holy Spirit). Do not deceive yourself. He will have the five talents and their increase ... Where are the souls you might have saved? Where are the children I would have given you? Where is the fruit?*

In the light of these ramifications, some of our bright lights are wrestling with this whole issue today. Some people think that soldiership is irreparably damaged and so they propose the institution of a holy order to fill the operational gap left by our desertion of covenant. They recognise that the Army needs dependable, trained, committed warriors ready to fight, but they forget that there are a million soldiers who have already covenanted with God. Others suggest that we create a lower level of membership so that the crowd on Sundays, not called or not willing to covenant with God, can still belong to the local corps congregation. However, a new lower level does nothing to address the tragic state of soldiership in some first-world locations or the loss of wonder-working, world-winning impact.

God, the restorationist

God is a restorationist. He is all about restoring broken relationships, restoring the years that the locusts have eaten, and restoring the promised land to His chosen people. The whole gospel is about God's plan to restore us to Himself. He goes to great lengths to bring about restoration. We know that His strategy to restore fallen humanity to relationship in His family took Him all the way to the Cross.

While there is nothing inherently wrong with holy orders and new levels of membership, God is a restorationist at heart. He wants you to restore your covenant with Him and it doesn't matter if the decision was made for the wrong motives. God isn't swayed by that argument. You may remember that Joshua made a bad covenant with the Gibeonites. After his brilliant success against Jericho the neighbouring Gibeonites were terrified and therefore determined to appease and deceive the powerful Israelites. Pretending to be from a far-away country they sued Joshua for peace. Joshua 'took of their victuals and asked not counsel at the mouth of the Lord' (Joshua 9:14, AV). Naively, he bought the mouldy bread and the cracked wineskins story but didn't even bother checking with God. It was an ill-formed covenant, but history shows us that God took this ill-formed covenant very seriously.

At least 150 years later Saul tried to wipe out the Gibeonites, thus breaking the forgotten covenant. It was probably forty years after this, under King David's reign, that God punished Israel with a lengthy famine for breaking this covenant. The high price in human lives, paid to restore peace after the broken covenant, is explained in 2 Samuel 21. God takes even ill-formed covenant seriously.

The revolutionary power of restored covenant

The potency of restored covenant is far beyond our comprehension. When we are living a sacrificial, committed lifestyle we have access to the promises of God. The gospel paradox, that only in slavery is there true freedom, liberates us to incite holy revolution around the world. In 1873, when the Army was still called The Christian Mission, George Scott Railton wrote:

> We are revolutionaries. We know that we have passed from death unto life, and we insist on the necessity of the same sweeping change in every human being.

Of course, salvation itself is a covenant relationship. When the Holy

Spirit at Pentecost unleashed the phenomenon called the Church, this Jesus thing went public. Persecution became an immediate expectation after conversion. No longer could leaders like Joseph of Arimathea follow Jesus in secret. He was outed by the drastic circumstances. No longer could people nurture private sins. The Holy Spirit exposed them, as with Ananias and Sapphira, and the costs were very high. No longer would religious people merely argue subtle complexities of the law. Old opponents like Pharisees and Sadducees would have to unite against a common foe whose success threatened their influence and lifestyle. No more was Caesar going to be able to count on the obeisance of the Jews. While converts would respect and obey the emperor, he took a back seat to their first and foremost fealty and obedience to their new King, Jesus Christ. No longer could casually religious Jews count on their Jewishness to save them. It would take repentance, and a public one at that.

The costs of disobedience to covenant are high

There was singleness of focus and purpose as covenanted disciples of Jesus gave up all to follow. As Kierkegaard understood purity to be 'willing one thing', so Commissioner George Scott Railton preached a covenant-holiness-inspired single focus:

> *Let us begin with a bold avowal of our flag, for we are not the children of darkness, but of light … Those who do not feel the urgent need of radical changes in themselves and in mankind, or those who cannot reconcile themselves to the desperate measures required by so desperate a case, have nothing in common with us. The world is lost, and Jesus has come to save it; and it must be saved, at any cost, and whatever that may require, because whoever is not saved will be damned forever.*

Ananias and Sapphira died for their sin, for their breach of covenant. A breach of covenant was regarded as a terrible sin (Ezekiel 17: 12-20). If covenant means literally 'to bind', then a breach of covenant is an unbinding, a breaking away from God. There can be no power when we break away from God. One of the most prolific songwriters of The Salvation Army was Herbert Booth, who never published a song after quitting the Army. Covenant is serious business.

It seems that whenever God is at war, He establishes an uncompromising standard for holiness. The costs of disobedience to covenant are high and the consequences of sin are immediate:

- So it was with Moses on the way to Egypt. God was evacuating His people. He insisted on circumcision for Moses' first-born son as a reminder of ownership and covenant. Failure to obey immediately almost cost Moses his life (Exodus 4: 25).

- So it was with Uzzah who tried to steady the tottering of the sacred ark (2 Samuel 6). God was establishing His presence in His capital as the ark of the law (or Ark of the Covenant) moved to Jerusalem. The people had been too familiar and casual with the presence of God, and God was restoring a sense of His holiness.

- So it was with Achan, who stretched God's rules and paid for it with his life, the lives of 36 otherwise innocent Israelite soldiers, and the lives of his extended family (Joshua 7).

From holiness to mission

When God is at war the consequences of sins are immediate. With covenant there is no room for compromise. We say that we want God to go to war in our midst, in our day. We say we want Him to mobilise a powerful Salvation Army, but are we prepared for the immediate consequences of sin, for the uncompromising standards of holiness? Are we afraid even to consider the changes called for long ago by Colonel John Dean?

Comrades, we want more prayer and less pride; more simple faith and

less self-sufficiency; more self-denial, less self-pleasing; more faithfulness,
less suavity; more regarding The Salvation Army as our Jerusalem and
less regard and attention to keeping good friends with Mammon.

The positive effects were worth it. In the day of Ananias and Sapphira masses were saved and the first army of God began to spread world-wide. The rewards remain worth it today. Our experience of holy covenant brings a trustworthiness freeing God to delight in us by releasing the Kingdom in fullness. Human enthusiasm takes us only so far. It peters out within a generation, and for most, after a busy weekend! The wild and outrageous doings of primitive (early) Salvationists would be relegated to history's footnote if they were but the humanly enthusiastic celebrations of earthly activity. Hear the Founder again:

If when slaves find freedom, and tradesmen make fortunes, and kindred,
or friends, or neighbours are delivered from some threatened calamity,
it is allowable to go mad with joy and to express it by hiring music, and
beating drums, and letting off fireworks, and shouting till hoarse, and
everybody says that is all right, then by the same rule, if you please, and
whether please or no, we are the slaves who now have our freedom, the
people who have made our fortune, we are the men who have seen our
kindred and friends and neighbours saved from damnation; and
therefore, we have a right to be merry.

As General William Booth explains here, our antics weren't mere human enthusiasm. They were inspired by holy influence on our lives. Now, covenant reins that enthusiasm. It purifies it from carnality and steers it right at our world-winning mission. That is the power of covenant. Covenant holiness can provide the trustworthiness required for God to pour out the fullness of His Kingdom. There is a Spiritless covenant that brings neither holiness nor power. Again Booth exposes that danger:

Rules and regulations are no use in themselves apart from the man. If
we could keep you all like volcanoes in a perpetual state of eruption, we

might dispense with them altogether. In heaven, I suppose there will be no commandments ... There will be no need for them.

I pray eagerly for the day when God unleashes the wonder-working, world-winning goodness and miracles that He has promised as part of His 'Greater Things' end-time package (John 14:12). William Booth felt the same way, when he exhorted us, 'By all means let us aspire after higher gifts' (*The War Cry*, March, 1885). Even more, let us aspire after a Father who is free to delight in us because He can trust us. It may be that we are akin to the people of Israel on the verge of entering the Promised Land. We've enjoyed the blessings of our heritage, but we've not proven trustworthy to receive the promised blessings ourselves. Those people had to enter their own covenant with God, being circumcised after crossing the Jordan (Joshua 5:3). Maybe we too, in order to establish a trust relationship with God that allows Him to delight in us and unleash through us the fullness of His Kingdom with wonder-working, world-winning power, need to take holy covenant more seriously, very seriously.

Let us cleave to our mission-reining covenant and fight in the freedom it offers us. From the Nazirite we inherit purity and power; from the Rechabite fidelity, loyalty, mobility, integrity, and a jealousy for the holiness of God, while all the time zealously warring to win the world for Jesus with a holy passion that never tires.

CHAPTER 12

MODERN-DAY 'PETERS'

HOLINESS AND LEADERSHIP STYLE

Commissioner Joe Noland

IF Jesus is perfection personified, Peter's life is perfection exemplified. Jesus, the quintessential spiritual leader, modelled holiness in the flesh. Peter, the revolutionary follower leader, exemplified this holiness following Pentecost. Both practised portable holiness thereby allowing their purity to mingle with depravity, to probe its vilest depths. Jesus moved into the neighbourhood and depravity was deprived of a series of lost souls – the sick, the lame, the unscrupulous, the deviants – a whole cast of dubious characters, outcasts and miscreants.

The Word became flesh and blood, and moved into the neighbourhood.
We saw the glory (holiness) with our own eyes, the one-of-a-kind glory,
like Father, like Son, generous inside and out, true from start to finish
(John 1:14, *The Message*).

Inclusive holiness modelled

Jesus is modelling a radically new understanding of holiness; the Pharisees and Scribes react against it; Peter is having a hard time coming to grips with it. The traditional view of holiness has a firm grip on Peter's psyche. It takes a hungry encounter on a rooftop, a descending sheet filled with 'non-kosher' (religiously unacceptable) food, and a visit to the house of a Gentile, Cornelius, before God dramatically gets Peter's attention (Acts 10).

Peter listens to Cornelius' story with God's descending revelation freshly reverberating in his mind – *Do not call anything impure that God has made clean.* Peter responds to Cornelius saying, 'I now realise how true it is that God does not show favouritism but accepts men from every nation who fear him and do what is right' (v.34, 35). Peter finally gets it! This was the defining moment – the turning point in Peter's spiritual leadership style. It was going to revolutionise the Church for centuries to come.

The traditional view of holiness might be called separatism. That is, all that is holy must be set apart from all that is unclean. In the Israelite tradition, never was anything that was holy supposed to meet or mingle with anything thought to be unclean. Consequently a great chasm grew between the Jewish church and the world. Peter had been indoctrinated with this kind of thinking. His was, for now, an exclusive religion, set apart for the chosen few.

Peter was not wrong to think that holiness means 'separation', because it does, but there is an important qualifier here and Peter, through the leading of the Holy Spirit, was able to grasp it. The distinction is this – Jesus separated Himself 'to' the world, not 'from' the world. He took His holiness *to* and *into* the world. When the visions of Peter and Cornelius collided on that fateful day, Peter was inspired and directed to exemplify these same patterns of holiness in his own leadership style. Holiness is never exclusive; it is always inclusive and, to quote William Sloan Coffin from his *Essays on Public Morality*, it is 'deeply ethical, never moralistic'.

Does our 21st century Church, and indeed The Salvation Army, need a new revolution, another defining moment, a turning point in its spiritual leadership style? If so, who will lead the way? Whose responsibility is it to step out front and, once again, model and teach this Peter-inspired brand of New Testament holiness? Can we be modern-day 'Peters'?

Portable holiness pioneered

To help answer these questions, let us go back to the early days of our movement. Diane Winston has written a book that explores the beginnings of The Salvation Army in New York City. In *Red-Hot & Righteous: The Urban Religion of The Salvation Army* she views the Army from a fresh and unbiased perspective. In the introduction she writes:

> I am not a Salvationist and I began with no brief for or against the movement. However, my research has given me a deep appreciation for the selfless work Salvationists have done and continue to do. Their compassion and dedication are truly compelling. In telling their story, I mean no disrespect by chronicling the changes that have shaped their

movement. Rather, I hope to demonstrate how religion finds new meaning and agency through its interaction with specific places and times.

When I was Territorial Commander of the U.S.A. Eastern Territory I had the opportunity of inviting Winston to meet and speak with our Territorial Executive Council. What amazed me most was her insightful grasp of the Army's primal heartbeat. She was able, succinctly yet profoundly, to define our uniqueness, that which has set us apart from other religious denominations and social service agencies. She got it! She is not even a Salvationist. With great literary skill, she very ably communicates the Army's uniqueness afresh. She describes how the Army made its holiness 'portable' and available to 'the whosoever', wherever.

In a chapter entitled 'The Cathedral of the Open Air', she quotes the following 1896 editorial from the pages of the *War Cry*:

The genius of the Army has been from the first that it has secularised religion, or rather that it has religionised secular things ... On the one hand it has brought religion out of the clouds into everyday life, and has taught the world that we may and ought to be as religious about our eatings and drinkings and dressing as we are about our prayings. On the other hand it has taught that there is no religion in a place or an attitude. A house or a store or factory can be just as holy a place as a church; hence we have commonly preferred to engage a secular place for our meetings ... our greatest triumphs have been witnessed in theatres, music halls, rinks, breweries, saloons, stores and similar places.

The 'genius of the Army' has been its bringing of holiness out into the secular market place. The 'genius of the Army' has been its separation 'to' the world, not 'from' the world. The 'genius of the Army' has been its modernisation of Peter's exemplary spiritual leadership style. If you read Diane Winston's book closely, you will find that she attributes the Army's success to the early outworking of its holiness theology:

> *Interpreting holiness theology as a way of being in the world,*
> *Salvationists made the entire city their mission field ... in divers*
> *neighbourhoods ... As Army leaders saw their lower-class constituency*
> *could not support such efforts (social services), they realised the need*
> *to communicate more than just a message of personal salvation.*

Now the questions beg themselves: What does this require of Christian leaders as they (some admittedly reluctantly and others unwittingly) face the challenge of a post-modern era? Does their leadership style exemplify the same brand of holiness modelled by those fearless pioneers of yore? Is the Army's birthright being challenged by its new-found exclusivity? Have our 'cathedrals of the open air' been replaced by 'sanctuaries extraordinaire'?

Mantle of leadership

As Jesus says, 'To whom much is given, much will be required' (Luke 12:48, NRSV). This still relevant axiom should speak volumes to a modern day Army and its leaders. When the mantle of leadership is bestowed, much is required. Peter's mantle took on new meaning when he got the picture – that he must adapt his holiness theology to a changing culture. This new message was not going to sit well with his traditional, exclusionary constituency. The purity of his living was going to be tested against the strength of his resolve. His life would be closely scrutinised, and his actions would be put to the test again and again. Peter triumphed; his leadership model is Holiness exemplified.

Since the days of the early Church, the world has become so much more complex and diversified. The population has exploded to 6 billion even as the planet continues to 'shrink', thanks to advances in technology and communication. In the Western world, the Army has enjoyed unprecedented acceptance from society and along with that, unparalleled material success. As modern-day 'Peters', the leaders of the Army face extraordinary challenges; the purity of their living will be tested against the strength of their resolve like never before.

While I am throwing around maxims, let us not forget this one: 'Be careful not to throw the baby out with the bath water.' The Army's holiness theology happens to be the 'baby' in this particular context. As it discards, as it rightly should, the bath water – mundane, irrelevant and outdated practices – its leadership must be ever mindful of that which has made and continues to make its ministry unique and successful, a holiness theology that is all-inclusive and very portable. Let the Army innovatively and aggressively adapt this never-changing holiness ethos to an ever-changing and increasingly demoralised world. In the process, let the Army continue to be 'deeply ethical, never moralistic'.

Leadership examples

There are some sterling examples of leaders who modelled this kind of holiness, but none so flamboyantly (at least in my time), as Commissioner Andy Miller. Henry Gariepy, in his book, *Andy Miller, A Legend and a Legacy*, illustrates through countless testimonials the inclusiveness and portability of Miller's practical holiness theology. In the introduction Gariepy quotes me as saying, 'Andy is my kind of leader, nothing contrived or disingenuous about him. He makes everyone he comes into contact with – beneficiary, door sergeant, lieutenant or commissioner – feel important. This is a rare gift.'

I witnessed this brand of holiness in action when Miller, as the Army's USA National Commander, accompanied the Santa Ana Band (where Doris and I were corps officers at the time) to a series of large Congress gatherings in Perth, Australia. This was the first time I had seen Andy Miller up close and personal. He would not allow Army protocol to interfere with his witnessing, mingling and soul winning. It was driving the territorial commander and divisional commander (who had everything well organised) crazy. When it was time to line up for the march of witness or formal entry into a meeting, Andy was never there. He could be found witnessing to street people or praying with the Lord

Mayor. *Rank, position* and *protocol* were not words found in his vocabulary. Gentile or Jew, poor or rich, it made no difference to Andy. Holy inclusiveness was the mantle he inherited, and adherence to procedures was not going to diminish the responsibility that came with it. Needless to say, it made a profound impression upon me.

Gariepy also wrote, 'With Andy there was no polarisation between the sacred and the secular. He viewed evangelism and practical ministry as obverse and reverse sides of the coin that makes up the Army. His brand of holiness was inextricably wedded to the hurts and needs of people around him. He was declaring the credo of Salvationists – that holiness without social concern is as a soul without a body, and social concern without holiness is as a body without a soul. One is a ghost, the other a corpse. Only when they are wedded together do we have a healthy, life-giving gospel.'

Andy literally took his holiness out into the marketplace.

We cannot all be Andy Millers, but we can, in our own inimitable ways, follow the example of Jesus. In the Gospels Peter, Matthew, John and Andrew did that, and they were as different as night and day. When Jesus chose His disciples, it was not an exercise in cloning. His was a relational gospel, so with many disciples relating to others in their own ways, variety is enhanced and the field of relational opportunities vastly enlarged. Jesus wants us to absorb that holy inclusiveness revealed to Peter into our own one-of-a-kind style and personality. He wants us to make holiness relevant to our time and circumstances.

Empowering the 'Power'

More importantly, as leaders (and all Christians are leaders to some degree) we have a responsibility to release and empower others for ministry, allowing our constituency to explore the full measure of His power in the execution of their ministerial duties. Portable holiness needs breathing room. It needs freedom to express itself. The whole Pentecostal experience was about empowerment. Jesus was not going to be around to hold His followers' hands anymore. He would not be there to bail them out of tight spots. There would be no directives pointing the way (other than the teachings they had already received). He wanted them to be as creative and innovative as possible. He understood that risk-taking would be part of their 'modus operandi'. He knew that failure was a prerequisite to success.

> *But you will receive power when the Holy Spirit comes on you; and you will be my witnesses in Jerusalem, and in all Judea and Samaria, and to the ends of the earth* (Acts 1:8).

He released and empowered them. The empowerment did not come in the form of another man or woman. It was the power of the Holy Spirit that took hold of that first group of leaders. There were no restrictions and there were no well-defined regulations to guide them. Peter, the very first Church leader, was emboldened by, and emblazoned with, this Power. It was he who first addressed that sceptical and quizzical crowd following Pentecost. He did not pull any punches and the message placed upon his lips cut to His hearers' hearts. New converts came into the fold. The disciples now became disciplers. Their leadership was critical at this juncture. This is what true leadership is, you see – discipleship. The Gospel could not have spread as quickly and widely as it did without this kind of empowerment. God, in the flesh, was limited. God, in the Spirit, is omnipresent. His omnipresence is magnified and glorified in and through the leadership of His followers – that's you and me.

Confusing the roles

As leaders we sometimes get the power roles confused, don't we? It's one of the weaknesses inbred in our humanity. We need to be reminded from time to time that we are not the power source; we are the Power's resource – Spirit filled instruments chosen to be the succeeding generation of God's disciples and anointed to lead, encourage and empower each new generation as it emerges.

As leaders today, are we not sometimes guilty of constraining the Power by insisting that it should fit neatly into prescribed, orderly, well-organised packages? It is true that people vary in their capacity to perform. It is true that some people need more direction than others. It is true that as an institution grows and develops, procedures and guidelines need to be developed. It is also true that the Holy Spirit works uniquely through the capacity and personality of each and every individual. Unfortunately, we often confuse 'direction' with 'control'; there is a distinct difference between the two. Let us never be guilty of controlling the flow of the Holy Spirit even though He may take an uncomfortable turn from time to time. Let us always be guilty of directing our people *into* that flow and helping them establish that critical 'holy balance' in their life and ministry.

Paradise flawed

In retirement I now find myself living vicariously through the ministry of my son, Rob, in Hawaii. He is pioneering a very non-traditional ministry in one of the more depraved, non-touristy sections of Oahu. It is paradise flawed, where, among other things, the abuse of the drug 'Crystal Meth' (also called 'ice') is rampant. Multiple generations are being tyrannised by its effect. This drug is a catalyst that exacerbates a plethora of other abuses and inequities that are victimising that culture and community.

Rob's sanctuary is the open air. Every Sunday morning he sets up a tent on the beach and worshippers come. The majority would never feel comfortable entering a traditional place of worship. Weekly Bible Studies are held on the beach under a tree; every morning at 7.00 a.m. he meets with 'the whosoever' for 'Devotions on the Ocean'. The uniform is slippers, shorts, and a specially designed T-shirt decorated with a flower lei wrapped artistically around the crest. On the sleeve is the name of the fellowship, 'Waianae Christian Ohana (Family)'. The centrepiece of the corps mission statement (formulated by the membership) is 'Come Just As You Are'. The 'Corps Standard' is not standard at all, but is very fluid; it changes with the directing flow of the Holy Spirit. Rob, with his wife, Denise, and two daughters has chosen to live in the community. The downstairs of their home becomes the gathering place for a whole host of ancillary activities, and they are doing this as employees with a modest stipend because they believe that this is where God wants them to be.

The 'genius of the Army' is alive and well in Waianae. The mantle of leadership has been passed on to Rob, and his holiness teaching is being soundly tested in a cultural setting where role models of the opposite kind are revered. I must tell you that this new message does not always sit well with an otherwise indoctrinated constituency. The space constraints of this essay do not allow me to delineate the many challenges that are his. Suffice it to say that the purity of his living is being tested against the strength of his resolve. His life is being closely scrutinised and his actions are being put to the test again and again. Through it all he has found the 21st century relevance of the 'genius of the Army' in this truism: The light of holiness shines brightest when it is taken into the darkest, coldest and vilest crevices of this world.

Do you get it?

I must also be quick to tell you that all of this would not be possible without the unequivocal support of Army leadership. Holiness is an individual thing, but it is also a corporate thing. God is calling us to personal holiness, and He is calling us to corporate holiness. One of the marks of holiness, one of the attributes of perfection is not only found in our relationship to Christ but also found in our relationship to others – how we receive them, how we treat them, how we encourage them (including those who serve under our leadership). Where is God's perfection? It is found in our personal and corporate response to others? It is not holiness constrained; it is holiness released. It is not holiness 'from' the world; it is holiness taken 'into' the world. It is not holiness controlled; it is holiness directed. It is holiness that is portable, adaptable and all-inclusive.

Jesus modelled it. Peter got it and modelled it. The Divisional Commander of the Hawaiian and Pacific Islands Division, Major Ralph Hood, gets it and is modelling it. Rob, the grass-roots employee, gets it and is modelling it. Their style of leadership is what I call, 'holiness exemplified'. Get it? Get it!

CHAPTER 13

IT IS OUR BUSINESS!

HOLINESS AND POLITICS

Captain Geoff Ryan

I have often been told that The Salvation Army is 'apolitical'. At best, this means that we do not engage in partisan politics. At worst, it means that we are unwilling to engage prophetically with the world around us or to challenge the unequal distribution of wealth and power in our society. Unless we see the implications of our faith for society at large, we risk becoming, as one author described Wesleyan Methodists, 'a religious order of political eunuchs' that teaches obedience to governing authorities, offers no political interference and would never countenance revolution (Dani Shaw, 'Politics and the Gospel', *Horizons* magazine, Canada, July/August 2003).

When Christians seek to exclude politics from their thinking they are bound to distort their theologies, for politics is an inescapable aspect of human existence, with direct relevance to the divine/human encounter (Philip Wogaman, *Christian Perspectives on Politics*).

1970 echoes

A S I watched the documentary a vague uneasiness crept over me. At first it was hard to define but the more I thought about it in subsequent days, the more a gradual understanding grew of what it was that niggled at me, causing me such unease. I have no idea how others with me felt. They may well have been helped and challenged by what they saw.

The film was a documentary about a relatively well-known revival that took place in 1970 at a Bible college in the United States. Theologically this college is in the same neighbourhood as The Salvation Army and in fact, there is a strong relationship between our denomination and this institute. A number of people who later grew to prominence as leaders in The Salvation Army were educated there. The film chronicles an event that started during a 10 am chapel service in the college's main auditorium on a February morning of that year. There was a visitation of the Holy Spirit that morning and He apparently decided to stay for a while. What was scheduled as a 50-minute chapel service turned into 185 hours of non-stop days and nights of weeping, repentance, singing, testimonies and prayer. The revival spread and by summer it had hit more than 130 other seminaries, Bible colleges and churches.

The video I watched consisted of a montage of clips and interviews shot at the time of the revival (even back then, it seems, evangelicals had the presence of mind to have a camera on hand) as well as more recent interviews with participants who recounted their reminiscences of what took place and what they believed it meant. Faculty members and students weighed in with their opinions and testimonies. There was a well-modulated soundtrack.

This revival video was being used across our Territory. It was shown at a number of the annual officer retreats as well as the Training College, where it seemed to have the effect of initiating a small series of minor mini-revivals with an emphasis on personal confession and repentance. It was shown, from what I could gather, in order to demonstrate what the Holy Spirit will sometimes do when He takes over; to show, in fact, what true revival can involve. It was used in conjunction with teaching on our doctrine and tradition of holiness, namely our second-blessing view of holiness as championed by Samuel Logan Brengle.

At the time I viewed the film at retreat I had coincidentally visited that very same college in the United States a year prior. Therefore I watched it with a point of reference in mind, albeit one that was thirty years after the event. Hence the uneasiness, I suppose. You see, when I visited the college, I found everything to be nice and polite, clean and organised. My hosts were courteous and hospitable to a fault and sincerity abounded. The initial 'flagging' came when I understood that the student body was about 98% white, overwhelmingly middle to upper-class and culturally – and by conviction – conservative (if not fundamentalist). So why the problem in me? Surely these students (and faculty) merely reflected the demographic make-up of North American evangelicalism in that particular part of the world. However, what I immediately noticed as I watched the revival video was that the crowd on the screen in front looked exactly like the same people I had rubbed shoulders with the year before. The hair styles and clothing fashions were a bit different, but otherwise it was like a time-warp and this caused me to lean forward, open my ears, focus my eyes and watch and listen very intently indeed to what was being presented to me.

Personal piety is not enough

It is difficult to explain, but it needs to be explained because for me it strikes at the heart of our present understanding of holiness and, by extension, the issue of faith and politics. In the evangelical/holiness tradition the tension lies smack in the middle between the exaltation and practice of personal piety and the Biblical imperative for social holiness, for a holiness too large and restless to be contained solely in individual human hearts. Revival (or at the very least renewal) has to do with the business of holiness, that is the holiness of God descending and making holy His people, but does it stop there? Does this imparted holiness primarily even reside there, content in the diminished role of simply burnishing up the hearts and rebooting the minds of the saints? If ultimately holiness and revival (a kind of Cupid and his arrow relationship) confine themselves to a privatised paradigm effecting little more than the sorting out of the personal and private sins of the saints (often the pale half-sins of generational Christians who have never really done anything particularly evil, nor anything spectacularly good), then how easily satisfied our God must be. I believe He has bigger fish to fry.

Yet this is what the revival video seemed to be about. It was limited to former students telling how, prior to the revival, they had been burdened with sins such as lying and pride; former faculty members confessing that they had been recalcitrant in adequately preparing for classes, and thereby guilty of disrespecting the calling God had given them and of a lack of love for their students and a lack of commitment to the task at hand. There were scores of people confessing a cavalier attitude toward worship, and prayer, and the things of the church.

Though only an infant when this revival took place, I know enough to realise that at that time in American society, as the turbulent 1960's moved into the 1970's, the old mores, customs and constructs were being radically challenged, fought and often mortally wounded. Old ways of 'doing business' were being trashed by a restless and discontented youth and this upheaval was being politically expressed primarily through two events: the escalating war in Vietnam, and the Civil Rights movement, epitomised by Martin Luther King Jr. who had been shot dead two years previously.

I do not know what the people in the film did with their lives in later years, but many contemporaries of these 1970 revivalists were getting themselves shot up and shipped home from South-east Asia in body bags. Others were taking to the streets to question and protest the fundamental justice of this conflict. Within three months the infamous Kent State riot would take place on another campus, resulting in four dead students. Peers of these college kids had marched beyond their fears to fall in step behind a charismatic preacher who led them into the maw of generations of prejudice and dehumanising hate. They faced injustice, poverty, class, race, war, and oppression and sought the place of a holy God amid all this very human mess. Here it was, all the truly vital biblical themes being played out on the streets and through the recruiting offices of that nation, but not a whisper of any of this even ghosted across the video screen. No mention of anything outside of themselves was recorded by any of the students or faculty, either at the time of the revival or three decades later. Yet here I was, in the very same institution, in the very same auditorium at a morning chapel service looking around, and seeing something that I thought should not have been. In a country that remains fractured largely along racial lines, it seemed to me that the blacks that followed Martin Luther King apparently have still not made it as far as the auditorium of this Christian institution. Neither had the poor. Reconciliation and inclusiveness seemed, on the surface of things, distant and alien concepts.

So I wondered (perhaps unfairly and unduly polemically as I am prone to do, and not knowing anything of what became of them in later life) why the Holy Spirit would choose to come and hang out with these Christians in order to give them what amounted to little more than a seasonal, spiritual tune-up? Why was this revival not the impetus for these students to move beyond the walls of their college chapel and into the fray with their black Christian brothers and sisters? Why was His convicting and purging presence not bivouacked down in the steamy jungles of Vietnam and spiralling out of the megaphones of the protestors as they were fired on by national guardsmen at Kent State? Why did He not bridge these worlds, why did He not bring them together, why confine Himself to this auditorium, to the resaving of people already fairly well saved and apparently not much of a mind to move out into the streets?

Did the revival that had such an impact that it became a seminal event in the lives of hundreds of future pastors and preachers (to the degree that it was memorialised on film some three decades later and employed as tinder to spark significant spiritual experiences for a number of my fellow officers) – did it move any of those students or faculty out of that auditorium and into the streets alongside their black brothers and sisters, or into the maelstrom of the Vietnam conflict, or into the corridors of political power in order to confront hate and injustice? Did holiness stream down, imparted from God into their hearts, causing 'justice to roll on like a river' in order to engage and change and transform a society with its hands at its own throat? Maybe I am judging too hastily and overstating my case. Possibly I am being unfair and overly sceptical, but I noticed a possible disconnect that day.

Is this really what holiness is about? Is this what revival means? Did not John Wesley, the spiritual father of the Holiness Movement and of The Salvation Army, claim that there is 'no holiness apart from social holiness'?

Booth and politics

During his years of active ministry, William Booth evolved from essentially a one-dimensional evangelist, interested in little more than saving souls in a spiritual sense (heavily influenced as he was by American revivalists such as Charles Finney and James Caughey) to an awareness, and then conviction, of the need for a hand-in-hand approach to evangelism and social service. He saw an holistic salvation – *No one gets a blessing if they have cold feet and nobody ever got saved while they had a toothache.* Furthermore, he moved to an eventual social ethic (best exemplified in his *In Darkest England and The Way Out*) to what Dr. Roger Green has termed a 'later theology of redemption'. By the time *In Darkest England* was published in 1890, the sixty-one-year-old Booth had undergone a definite paradigmatic shift. He had moved beyond social service into social reform and therefore, of necessity, into the political realm. Booth's 'cab horse charter', overseas farm colonies, legal aid offices, employment agencies, the Army's engagement with the poor laws and with the change in legislation regarding the age of consent, the 'Lights in Darkest England' match factory which resulted in changes to labour law changes and workers' rights legislation – this was ultimately all political stuff. It was about challenging unjust laws, changing legislation, and assailing structures that cripple and shorten lives and warp and twist souls.

The infamous 'White Slave' scandal is axiomatic. In 1885 Bramwell Booth, son of William Booth and then the Army's Chief of the Staff, in conjunction with W.T. Stead, editor of the *Pall Mall Gazette*, conspired to stage the purchase of a thirteen-year-old girl, one of the thousands of girls sold annually in London into prostitution. A sensational series of articles on the 'White Slave Trade' was published in the *Pall Mall Gazette* and the resulting scandal threatened the very existence of The Salvation Army and of the *Gazette*. A price was paid by most of the people involved in the plan, including time served in prison. Bramwell, however, did not serve time in jail and The Salvation Army's prestige soared as a result of this incident. Riding the tremendous wave of publicity generated by the case, the Army presented Parliament with a petition of 393,000 signatures demanding that the age of consent be raised to fifteen. Within two weeks the government had bowed to the pressure and voted to raise the age of consent to sixteen. Booth stated in the *War Cry*: *We thank God for the success He has given to the first effort of The Salvation Army to improve the laws of the nation.*

As far as I am concerned, that is politics. Maybe these days we would more accurately describe this as 'direct action'. Certainly it moved well beyond the bounds of advocacy or lobbying. Just the same, the end result was an involvement with the political process that resulted in change. It was involvement due to a pressing social injustice. The motivation was to right a wrong. This pattern has subsequently been repeated in Army operations in various other countries. In 1900 Colonel Henry Bullard and Captain Gumpei Yamamuro forced the Japanese government to sign legislation crippling the slave trade in women prostitutes in the walled city of Yoshiwara in the middle of Tokyo. In 1938, due to the efforts of Ensign Charles Péan, the French authorities closed down the notorious prison colony in French Guiana known as 'Devil's Island'. Many similar stories could be told.

Tony Campolo, the American sociologist and speaker, makes the case that it is all well and good to be constantly the good Samaritan, always willing to stop and pick up the wounded, to look after them, get them better and save them. However, after the tenth robbery victim is picked up, maybe it is time to see what can be done about making the road from Jerusalem to Jericho a bit safer. The smart thing, ultimately, is to move from reactionary, band-aid solutions to pro-active preventive strategies that of necessity deal with structural and often legislative injustices. Inevitably there comes the time to engage with the political system that permits, and often facilitates, such wrong. This was the journey that I believe Booth underwent from 'pure' evangelist to redemptive theologian.

No privatised holiness

The holiness doctrine that was being preached in the rented music halls and borrowed stables and tents that were home to our Salvationist forbears, was understood from the beginning (initially instinctively and then, progressively, philosophically and theologically) as having import for the whole person and by implication, the whole of society. Whatever spin on the gospel these 'corybantic Christians' were putting on matters, it was definitely not an espousal of privatised religion. The early years of The Salvation Army, with its hard and unflinching holiness apologetic, constituted a true revival. It was counter-cultural to the accepted wisdom of western Christianity of that time and place which practised a privatised and individualistic religion (a notion that would see its full flowering in late, twentieth century evangelicalism). Those early Salvationists would have been in agreement with the views of George Lyons in his lecture 'Is Holiness Contagious?' at the Northwest Nazarene College, on April 4, 1995:

We have conceded to the non-biblical view that there are some areas of life that are not God's concerns, that there are sacred and secular realms of life. Jesus rejected the notion that any area of life was outside the sovereignty of God. But we have privatised holiness so that Christians have increasingly lost influence in the political, economic, scientific, and moral spheres of human life. We have relegated holiness to our private inner lives. Wholesome intentions matter more than holy living.

The Bible is a political book. Christianity is a social faith. The Salvation Army was conceived as an urban, social justice movement. Any expression of spirituality manifested by any people of God that avoids political engagement, that is excessively privatised and inwardly-focused, that operates without an intentional activism and keen awareness of the essential injustice of the world, is a betrayal of biblical Christianity. For us it is also a betrayal of our Salvationist heritage. Any such expression of holiness is bound to be but a pale shadow of God's intentions, if not full heresy.

Mainstream evangelicalism is generally content to view charitable acts, social assistance and the fighting of injustices (and by extension engagement with the political realm) as mere adjuncts to holy living. They are things we *do* rather than core aspects of God's nature and thus our attempts to conform to Him. In conventional belief and practice, the main game is played out between God and us, within our hearts and souls and minds and the benefits that might be passed on to someone else due to our personal journey of faith is at best a by-product, seen as no more than an incidental thing effected primarily to prove to God our love and devotion. We practise a vertical relationship when in fact true holiness is a Trinitarian construct. As Commissioner Phil Needham states: *We tend to see the relationship between holiness and community as one-directional ... I am convinced that the key to our wholeness as a salvation people is the marriage of holiness and community.* Needham cites the privatisation of holiness as one of the main obstacles to a true understanding of holiness and asserts that sanctification involves the restoration of community (Ephesians 2:13-17; 3:2-6; 4:12-16).

If holiness is to be viewed as a personal journey, it is only insofar as it is seen as part of a journey in fellowship with other believers (Ephesians 2:19-22, 1:4-5, 10b). Brengle himself taught that holiness is meaningless without its corporate expression (Ephesians 4:1-6) and General Frederick Coutts said that holiness can only be realised in and through relationships (Ephesians 4:25-32; 5:21ff). The key, according to Needham, is the integration of holiness and community as found in the doctrine of the Trinity. Politics is, as Philip Wogaman states, *an inescapable aspect of human existence, with direct relevance to the divine/ human encounter.*

The Evangelical Revival that took place in England in the first half of the 1700's under George Whitefield and John Wesley (1703-91) has been credited with saving England from the same sort of Revolution (1789) that France was later to go through. Whether this is really the case will remain a matter of debate and speculation for historians. Indisputable however, is the fact that this revival cut across denominational lines and touched politically every class of society. It took a stand against slavery and supported William Wilberforce in his crusade. Out of the revival arose numerous agencies promoting Christian, charitable work – antislavery societies, prison reform groups, relief agencies for the poor. Hospitals and schools multiplied. The social, cultural and political impact of the holiness theology that Whitefield and Wesley preached is inestimable. It did not confine itself to Christian churches and institutions alone and it did not confine itself solely to the private spiritual struggles of individual Christians. It engaged with the toughest issues of the day and transformed a nation. It seems to me that this is the mark of true revival and this must be the legacy that holiness would leave.

A political Army?

Without engagement in the lives of people and the affairs of government that directly affect the life and destinies of people, our holiness will only ever be a distorted theology and a spiritually stagnant pool. The inevitable outcome of excessive pietism is to end up something like the Amish – rigorously holding on to what we believe to be the ordinances of holiness in order to keep our own selves unspotted and pure, but in the meantime moving so far outside the pale of relevancy that we become a historical curiosity at best, an irrelevant oddity at worst. The purity and holiness we are exhorted to seek throughout the pages of Scripture is primarily for the sake of others. It is not for God's benefit. He is complete and self-contained and needs nothing from us. It is not for the church's benefit. The church exists for those outside the church (The Salvation Army even more). It is not for our personal benefit. If we seek to save our lives, we will lose them, as we are told clearly by Jesus. We are to be holy for the sake of an unholy world, for the sake of a lost, hurting, dying world. *Down these mean streets must come a man who himself is not mean, neither is he tarnished nor afraid*, wrote the novelist Raymond Chandler. This is as good an argument for the necessity of God's people seeking holiness in, and for the sake of, the world that I have ever heard.

Traditionally The Salvation Army has posited a non-partisan, apolitical stance. This is a nod to expediency more than anything else. In Orders and Regulations for Officers the section on 'Governments, Public Authorities and other Societies' is fairly sparse and rather vague. The essential tenets are a neutrality in matters of party politics (which might mean one thing in benign and politically comatose Canada but quite another in the deadly turmoil of Liberia) and an implicit understanding that the Army enters politics only with regard to matters of social need and the welfare of people. Our non-partisan policy is a good thing. Legally, as a charity, we are bound in many countries to such a course. Ethically, we realise that no one political party or persuasion has a complete handle on the truth and so for us to throw our lot in with one party over and against another would be limiting and foolish. We would quickly lose our ability to speak prophetically. When, however, this non-partisan stance becomes an apolitical refusal to engage with the issues of the day and the political process that orders such issues, or if we settle for a comfortable 'moral neutrality', then it is bad.

I understand that the decision the Army made to embrace party political neutrality was not at first theologically motivated, but an organisational and, in point of fact, political decision. It became practice not fundamentally out of conviction but out of structural and managerial necessity (read as risk management and damage control). It was a concession that our Founders felt they needed to make for the sake of the Army's growing internationalism. This was one of the prices to be paid if the Army was truly to circle the globe, as Booth's vision demanded. As more countries came under our yellow, red and blue flag the implications of overt political allegiance and engagement in any localised context became increasingly seen as a liability with unacceptable consequences. The stand that the Army might take in one country could make it worse for Army personnel and operations in another part of the world.

I ran into this dilemma numerous times while serving overseas in Russia where we often found ourselves in delicate situations as a foreign organisation, usually on the defence against the culturally dominant expression of faith (the Russian Orthodox Church) which wielded tremendous political power in post-perestroika Russia. Like dominoes, it so often seemed that any move made anywhere would have a repercussive effect, usually negative, in other parts of Russia, not to mention the surrounding countries of Georgia, Moldova and the Ukraine. The political winds needed to be tested daily.

As with The Salvation Army's position on the sacraments, most of the 'policy' decisions that have shaped our modus operandi as a church and mission have eventually required theological justification and rationale and these were generally sought as after the fact qualifiers. The motivating impetus for the change of our positions and practices was often mitigating circumstances, operational expediency and 'real politic'. The question that needs to be asked today, therefore, is whether or not the time has come to make a change, both in policy and practice, with regard to our apolitical posture? Should The Salvation Army become more politically active at local, national and international levels? Should officers be permitted, for example, to run for political office? Should we employ the cachet that we accumulated over the past 130 plus years of existence and place it on the line, if need be regardless of consequences, if the cause is right? Will we be the religious Levite on that road to Jericho, the Good Samaritan, or something else altogether?

The examples usually cited of Jesus shying away from political involvement are: Satan's temptation of Him on the mountaintop; the jubilant crowd seeking to make Him king; Pilate questioning Him and His reply that His kingdom was not of this earth. In each case it was power that Jesus was rejecting, a power that was being falsely offered on the premise that it be misused.

I have never really been able to understand how anyone can believe in the possibility of compromise in matters of power, which is an absolute passion according to Malcolm Muggeridge. Yet power always comes into the dynamic when we speak of politics. This seems at odds with our Christian sensibilities, yet the power to do good is a necessary tool in a fallen world. If power is going to be wielded (and it is) would it not be better for it to be wielded by holy people in the service of good? If holiness in its essence is a community affair, a matter concerned with relationships both within the family of God and to the world that God 'so loved' (John 3:16), and if the political structure is the primary means whereby order is established and maintained in society, then cannot the absence of God's people, of Salvationists, in this landscape be construed as a gross sin?

Can we afford to remain non-partisan? If we do, can we claim to be a holy people at all?

CHAPTER 14

IN THE STEPS OF THE PIONEER

HOLINESS AND ROLE MODELS

Captain Matt Clifton

'Rusty-James,' Steve said. I didn't look up. Steve sounded like he felt sorry for me and I didn't want to see him feeling sorry for me, because if I did I would hit him, no matter what. 'You're just like a ball in a pinball machine. Getting slammed back and forth; and you never think about anything, about where you're going or how you're going to get there…' I didn't understand what he was talking about. I did think about where I was going. I wanted to be like the Motorcycle Boy. I wanted to be tough like him, stay calm and laughing when things got dangerous. I wanted to be the toughest street fighter and most respected hood on our side of the river. I had tried everything … Even though nothing had worked so far, that didn't mean nothing ever would.

W E cannot help it. Certain other people, living and dead, ignite dreams in us – dreams that consume our hearts and minds irresistibly, like a forest fire. Like Rusty-James in S.E. Hinton's novel, *Rumble Fish*, we instinctively seek out role models.

Rusty-James dreamed, as we all dream. He dreamed of laughter in the face of danger, of being the local hero in the image of his elder brother, the Motorcycle Boy. Amid cold realities – his lack of direction, his reliance on fists over brains – the fire of his dreams gave him vital warmth. In this he is universal. We all know of a potential not yet reached and a life not yet lived. Unless dampened by despair, that awareness becomes tinder to sparks of hope. Dreams are then sure to ignite within us – it is instinctive; it is survival.

Rusty-James was, in the words of Anais Nin, 'in a process of becoming'. His were the admissions of John Newton: 'I am not what I would like to be; I am not what I hope to be.' We who long for holiness go further with Newton: 'I am also not what I ought to be.' We are the most discontent of all people, for the command of God – 'Be holy' – has ignited a dream within us of a life bursting at the seams with selfless love. It is a dream too glorious to resist. We have seen Jesus and found ourselves, as Frederick Coutts said, unable to unsee.

Rusty-James dreamed, as we all dream, but his dreams turned to ashes. His role model was a signpost to nowhere, unable to keep him from getting slammed back and forth until he blindly took a series of wrong turns to disaster. We, however, in our discontent, are paradoxically also the most hopeful. Jesus has pioneered a sure path and has also become our destination. As we travel, we find signposts, certain other people, living and dead, who stoke up the dream because it has become real, albeit partially, in their lives.

We are unique individuals, and God has mapped out unique journeys for us. My purpose in this essay is to help you seek out the signposts, unique to you, that will compel you to fix your eyes on your destination, the Pioneer and Perfecter of our faith – Jesus.

'A great cloud of witnesses'
The importance of diverse role models

While many of us would like it to be otherwise, diet is important. We have to eat, and what we eat has a direct impact on our health. Spending time writing tempts me to consume nothing but coffee and cookies, but I need the discipline of a balanced diet! In the same way, our diet of role models has a direct impact on our spiritual life. We need a dynamic balance, a creative tension, as we become exposed to the influence of other people. For me that means exposure to my mother's intuitive sensitivity while soaking up my father's pragmatic wisdom. That helps me be holy in both listening and speaking.

We Salvationists are often to be found devouring books that take us to our roots. Troubled by the famine of our own day, we revel in the feasting of early soul-winners – Railton, Cadman, Booth-Tucker, Brengle, and of course, the Booths. In biographies like Richard Collier's *The General Next to God* and Bernard Watson's *Soldier Saint*, we find qualities that stir our passion for holiness. Give me Catherine Booth's fierce purity and Railton's creative daring!

Immersion in our origins, when the Holy Spirit was so lavishly poured out, is essential. However, it is possible to overdose on such material. The early pioneers were children of their time, and the peculiarities of our day demand a different kind of saint. Who is living the holy life in

188

the real world today? Who is successfully attracting others to Jesus today? Seek them out! Watch them! Listen to them!

In the corps where I became a soldier of the Army in my early twenties, I watched my commanding officer lose his wife to cancer. I witnessed his agony first-hand. I also heard this outstanding pastor surge with compassion in the sermons following his loss. As soon as I felt its effects, I wanted that quality. A dream ignited. Because of that officer, and others, I am an officer today. No amount of Salvationist biography could have provided such an experience. Pursue a creative tension between saints past and present, and between saints in the books and saints in the flesh.

Another danger with immersion in Salvationist biography is that it majors on evangelical activism. While justly proud of who we are, we must also see that ours is but one narrow current within a very wide river of spirituality. We have much to learn. These are days when activism has its shortcomings. I can remember when futurists predicted that the greatest problem of the twenty-first century would be what to do with all our leisure time! There is a lamentable comedy about this prediction, at a time when personal computing power doubles every year. As technology gets faster, we live faster, and pay increasing homage in nervous tension to our inventions. We are enslaved, not liberated. This is not a time to lean wholly on the activism of the past. It is too hard to find Salvationists today who are role models in resting and the discipline of private prayer. One early Salvationist biography is still the only book I have read that openly dismisses the need for prayer in solitude. While we do have Army role models – the poet, Catherine Baird, springs readily to mind – is this not a time when we need to drink in also the influence of other Christian traditions rich in mysticism and contemplation? History abounds with saints who have radiated peace in the midst of unrest and aggression. If Jesus gives us peace of a quality unmatched by the world (John 14:27), then we sin if we do not have it. There are role models who will help us receive.

I would go further still and urge exploration of role models beyond our faith. The undoubtedly exclusive declaration of Jesus, 'I am … the truth' (John 14:6), did not bequeath to His church a monopoly on truth. I am happy to allow anyone to influence and inspire me whose qualities point me to Jesus. First we must know and esteem Jesus above all others. Then, with intelligent discernment, we may delve profitably into the riches of all humanity. Among the most eminent non-Christian role models is Mahatma Gandhi. A Hindu who embraced other faiths and had a profound admiration for Jesus, Gandhi gained a number of Christian admirers. When Christians debate who will be in heaven, Gandhi's name seems to crop up more than any other! Through biography and film, his life can still inspire, and indeed, rebuke us.

We walked towards a little village which was a mere collection of flyblown and squalid shacks. 'This is the real India,' said the voice beside me. As we stood there I noticed four or five men were squatting in front of us. They were relieving themselves. I glanced around me: what I had taken to be the droppings of dogs was, I realised, all human excreta. It was outside the hovels, it was beside their only well… Gandhi stood silent. A look of intense pity and sorrow came into his face. With the same expression of abject humility as though he himself was personally to blame for all this suffering and filth, he began to scavenge the excreta and bury it with his own hand. As we did this together, the villagers at first stood by and watched. Then the example of their beloved Mahatma worked upon them. Within a few minutes, the villagers began to follow his example. Gandhi's act of selfless action, of service, had achieved in a moment what coercion or teaching could not have done in a century.

It is always a great relief when, having accidentally taken wrong turns, we find a signpost that points us once again to our journey's end. Are your role models diverse? If they are all male, or all female, or all Salvationists, or all Protestants, or all long-dead saints from history, you may be making it hard for yourself to stay on track. Are you still in sight of the signposts that will help you travel swiftly and surely to Jesus?

'Say it ain't so, Joe'
When role models fail

Joseph Jefferson Jackson was the stuff of sporting legend – a poor, illiterate boy from the country who rose to baseball stardom as the First World War ended. Among Chicago gangsters and boozers, clean-living and clean-hitting Joe shone out as a hero. However, Shoeless Joe had feet of clay. 'Say it ain't so, Joe.' Legend has it that the famous plea came from a tearful urchin as Joe and seven team-mates left a trial accusing them of deliberately throwing the 1919 World Series. The plea sums up the heartache known by anyone who has looked up to someone, and then finds himself unexpectedly looking down.

Like Joe Jackson, few people ask to be role models. We should be careful, lest the high and precarious pedestals we place people on cause them to fall. A healthy eagerness to seek out role models should be tempered by an awareness of the basic fragility of people, however strong and secure they are in Christ. They may fail us, and our journey needs to continue unhindered. However, failure forms an avenue for grace, and God may fix up a broken signpost at a different junction. The veteran enemies of the soul like to gather there – discouragement, condemnation and despair among them. Watching someone do battle and break free is a help to holiness in itself. That is why David, one of the great biblical role models, is as valued for Psalm 51 as he is for 1 Samuel 17.

Acknowledging universal fragility connects us with Paul's wisdom. In teaching about the Body of Christ, he stressed that 'those parts of the body that seem to be weaker are indispensable' (1 Corinthians 12:22), and that 'its parts should have equal concern for each other' (1 Corinthians 12:25). I recall the example of an officer who greatly admired a retired colleague, a Commissioner, who had given exemplary missionary service. In extreme old age, and in the raw grief of his wife's death, the senior officer leant heavily on the secure belief in heaven of his younger admirer. The time may come when the tables are turned and when your role model needs you.

Notwithstanding universal fragility, God has provided a glorious wealth of holy people whose lives point us to Jesus. These are merely signposts, however, and we should never mistake them for our destination. For young Christians especially, it might be tempting to over-invest hopes and dreams in a living person. Flesh and blood charisma can intoxicate the senses and disorient the soul. Yet Jesus still refuses to compete with wind, earthquake and fire. The roar subsides, as it must. Then He comes, and with a whisper, reorients the soul heavenward.

'Follow me!'
Jesus, the role model

I received an unexpected call recently from a friend and retired officer – a role model. He is a radiant man, a quality that somehow traverses the telephone wires. His words were ointment. They touched needs he knew nothing about – secret struggles, wounds. As if compelled, he repeated over and over words from Hebrews 12:2, 'Fix your eyes on Jesus.' This is the disciple's maxim – the best advice ever given.

We are to see Him as He endures the Cross. The appeal is for an undivided gaze. The accent – He is simply called '*Jesus*' – is on His humanity. He has identified with us and He is like us, in order that we might be like Him. Among the many passions that energise Salvationists, none is more elemental than this. Holiness is Christlikeness. The dream, ignited and always burning, is to be like Jesus.

Yet we cannot be like Him if He is unlike us. Several images of Jesus were publicly displayed and a poll taken on the question: which picture looks most like Jesus as you imagine Him to be? Among examples from icons, paintings and stained glass windows, two pictures took the votes. One was a photograph of the actor Robert Powell from the 1977 film 'Jesus of Nazareth'. The other was a sketch of Jesus laughing. It was as if the question had been: which picture do you most relate to? It seems we imagine Him according to our need. Not a distant Christ – haloed, iconic and blandly serene. Our need is for One clothed in the chaos of our world, which is often beautiful, but also vile and grotesque.

He is Immanuel – God with us – the God we need. Yet the writer to the Hebrews, who so urgently directs our gaze to the human face of God, adds a qualifier. We learn that Jesus 'had to be made like his brothers in every way' (Hebrews 2:17) to free us from death's power, to atone for our sins and to help us in temptation. Then we are led to understand that Jesus was 'tempted in every way, just as we are – yet was without sin' (Hebrews 4:15). There it is! The word 'yet' marks a gap – some would say chasm – between Jesus and us. He never sinned, yet we all have. Universal fragility has a unique exception.

Is the dream futile? Do we yearn for an impossible ideal? Or can we leap the chasm? Is a full experience of His life offered to us, even life without sinning? We touch here on the thorniest problem in holiness doctrine. This problem must be faced if following Jesus is to produce transformation instead of frustration.

'Free indeed?'
The question

On this question the most eminent teachers sharply diverge. Standing in a lineage that includes such greats as the Booths, Charles Finney and the Wesleys, Salvationists still lift up the possibility of life without sinning, at least officially (see Appendix 7, *Salvation Story*, the most recent 'Handbook of Doctrine'). However, we find it hard to be secure when this is strongly denied by popular writers such as Philip Yancey and Jerry Bridges, who inherit a legacy that includes Bishop J. C. Ryle (the leading Anglican contemporary of the Booths) and reaches back to the Puritans.

The scriptures are tantalisingly ambiguous, which accounts for the problem. On the one hand, the promise of John 8:34-36 could hardly be more explicit: 'I tell you the truth, everyone who sins is a slave to sin. Now a slave has no permanent place in the family, but a son belongs to it forever. So if the Son sets you free, you will be free indeed.' When added to teaching from Romans 6 and 1 John 3, with an emphasis on the power of the atonement and the baptism with the Holy Spirit, the case seems made. Yet 1 John 1:8 is equally clear: 'If we claim we have not sinned, we make him out to be a liar and his word has no place in our lives.' When the appeal is added to see ourselves in the honest anguish of Romans 7, the opposing case gains a compelling power.

Underlying the problem is the challenge of defining sin and sinning. Is all sin 'conscious' – outcomes of the will – or are there sins that we are unconscious of? Teachers talk of the 'seriousness of sin', 'sins committed in ignorance' in Leviticus, and the experience of the Holy Spirit 'revealing sins that we were not previously aware of'. Yet as we move from the Old to the New Testament, the locus of accountability moves from the law to the heart, by which we mean the will – the seat of our motives and intentions. I confess to finding it hard to reconcile 'unconscious sin' with divine justice. I think of those whose actions have been disconnected from the will – those for whom Jesus surely has particular compassion. I think of the mentally ill, or of the saints who curse and become aggressive as senile dementia sets in. Have they really become sinners again?

Then there is the grey area between conscious and unconscious actions. While I find the idea of 'unconscious sin' abhorrent in its implications for the most damaged and vulnerable of people, I also find no solace in John Wesley's neat definition of sin as 'a voluntary transgression of a known moral law'. Much as I would like to, I simply cannot divide my deeds into black and white lists of the deliberate or accidental. The regrettable things I do arise from a complex fusion of will and weakness, where the will itself is an alchemy of selfless and selfish motives that defies analysis. I cling to the hope that I am capable of genuine selflessness. Some would counsel that even my tears of repentance need to be washed, yet I cannot say that my motives are never pure. The problem is that I simply do not know myself well enough to be certain.

'I am the truth'
The experiences of Jesus

Jesus said, 'I am the truth' (John 14:6). Truth is embodied in a Person and is not confined to propositions or to neat lines of logic. I have begun to learn that solace comes not from a definition, but from a life, a role model. For in His sinlessness, Jesus is both the problem and the answer. Implicit in the stark Gospel accounts of His life is all of the complex ambiguity that is the common currency of humanity. In the centre of it all, there resides an exquisite purity.

The temptations in the desert provide perhaps the clearest window, if we bear in mind the dynamics of temptation. Temptation is not temptation unless it plays upon powerful, elemental desires with guile and seduction. Jesus must have experienced those desires, together with the possibility of giving way to them. We must somehow envisage that He could have violated His identity within the Godhead, or else the account of his temptations is meaningless. What were those desires? Greed, lust for power, rebellion, and autonomy are all evident. Since He was *'tempted in every way, just as we are'*, we must add to these all the coins in common currency – pride, jealousy, aggression, and most definitely sexual temptation, much as reverence inclines us to recoil from the idea.

Gethsemane provides another window on the human face of God, where temptation exploits fear in a battle for the will. This again is common currency. The King of kings is not cosseted in the royal box, but has stepped into the arena to take the blows, to parry and thrust, to spill blood, and ultimately to emerge utterly exhausted, yet victorious. It is amid the chaos of not knowing ourselves fully, of not knowing our foe fully, of wrestling with the complex ambiguities of being human, that we need victory.

'Free indeed!'
Assurance

I recall a conference where I sat under holiness teaching that disappointed me. In the good cause of pastoral honesty, it seemed as though, in the teaching presented, a pact with sin had been made – a concession to its prevalence and power. I had been reading Catherine Booth's *The Highway of our God* where she pleads for the holiness standard to be upheld. She was a prophet. I knew that her written legacy was warning me about what I had just heard. I needed to take a walk alone. I paced back and forth along the edge of a lake, struggling to reconcile the well-meant teaching with my intense, burning dreams. Instinctively, I lifted the burden of my inner battle to God. The response was indescribably beautiful. Still dews of quietness fell. Jesus drew near and simply said to me, 'You are pure.' When He speaks, no conflicting voice can steal His authority.

What I received was not doctrinal clarity, but *assurance*. That is why I want to emphasise that solace comes essentially from relationship, not teaching. John 8:31-32 shows us that the task of teaching is to nurture the intimacy with Jesus that brings freedom. Yes, 'the truth will set you free', but remember that Truth is a Person, not a proposition! I cannot produce from Scripture easy, watertight definitions and doctrines to prove that we can be kept from sinning, but my heart adores and yearns for what my mind cannot contain. Scripture nurtures my hopes and dreams. Scriptural teaching leads me into experience – the assurance of victory that Jesus alone brings.

Practically, this means taking time to be nourished by scripture, especially the Gospels. The best advice once again is 'Fix your eyes on Jesus', and learn from His practice of solitude. Reread His promises in the early morning, and be sustained in them through the day. If failure comes, confess it and move on. Never yield an inch to discouragement. Look to the pastoral support of verses like 1 John 2:1 or Hebrews 4:15-16.

Assurance brings freedom to follow the Pioneer of our faith as He lives a life bursting at the seams with selfless love. John 13:1-17 reveals just how sharp and exhilarating the challenge is. Here is our role model setting an example (v15); showing us the full extent of His love (v1). He begins by humiliating Himself. Foot washing would have been too demeaning even for a Jewish slave. This lowest of tasks was carried out by Gentiles. Yet here was their beloved Master crouched down before them. No wonder Peter spluttered his objection! Verse 2 is calculated to strike the heart: 'The evening meal was being served, and the devil had already prompted Judas Iscariot, son of Simon, to betray Jesus.' Knowing this, Jesus knelt down and lovingly tended to the feet of Judas. Would you and I have found the strength to do the same?

Reflection – frequent, prayerful re-reading – cannot fail to shape the heart, fuel the dream, and bring assurance. What greater goal than to pursue with single-minded determination the likeness of Jesus Christ, and then finally to reach our destination? *'Dear friends, now we are children of God, and what we will be has not yet been made known. But we know that when he appears, we shall be like him, for we shall see him as he is'* (1 John 3:2).